THE FILMS OF
WOODY ALLEN

Acknowledgements

Stefano Jacini, Giuliana Nicodemi, Lucius Barre, Gail Sicilia, Patrizia Ugolotti, Nicoletta Grill, Gisa Lipowec and Margherita Uras of the USIS in Milan, Leo Pasqua, Franco Ciusa, Annamaria Mojetta and Lois Abrams have each in their own way encouraged and made possible the realisation of this book.
I owe it to them to express here my sincere gratitude and highest regards.
The copyright in the photographs is held by the various film distribution companies which have been kind enough to supply them, or by Woody Allen himself. Certain ones come from the archives of the weekly Sorrisi e canzoni TV, *who have kindly put them at my disposal.*

Giannalberto Bendazzi

Translated by Paul and Christopher Clark and
edited by Colin Clark

This edition published by Ravette Limited, 1987
Ravette Limited
3 Glenside Estate, Star Road
Partridge Green, Horsham, Sussex RH13 8RA, England

Printed in Italy by Gruppo Editoriale Fabbri, Milan

ISBN 1 85304 000 2

THE FILMS OF
WOODY ALLEN

G. BENDAZZI

Ravette London

Contents

A Life of Woody Allen   5
Anti-Hero Woody Allen   29
The Films of Woody Allen   43
Take The Money And Run   44
Bananas   54
Play It Again, Sam   66
Everything You Always Wanted To Know About
   Sex, But Were Afraid To Ask   76
Sleeper   86
Love And Death   96
Annie Hall   110
Interiors   122
Manhattan   132
Stardust Memories   148
A Midsummer Night's Sex Comedy   158
Zelig   168
Broadway Danny Rose   180
The Purple Rose of Cairo   186
Hannah And Her Sisters   192
Radio Days   198
Films   204
Records, Books, Plays, Bibliographical Notes   206
Index of Names   207

A Life of
WOODY ALLEN

United States, 1935. President F. D. Roosevelt announces the 'Second New Deal', to combat the economic depression which has lasted since 1929. Henry Miller publishes *Tropic of Cancer*, and John Steinbeck *Tortilla Flat*.

Detroit wins baseball's World Series, but even this is less important than the transfer of the great Babe Ruth from the New York Yankees to the Boston Braves. Jim Braddock becomes world heavyweight boxing champion, succeeding Max Baer and Primo Carnera. In Hollywood, the Oscars are awarded in February: a triumph for Frank Capra and his *It Happened One Night*. The first 'real' colour film, *Becky Sharp* by Rouben Mamoulian, is released. Also released are *The Informer* by John Ford, *The Devil Is A Woman* by Josef Von Sternberg, starring Marlene Dietrich, *Anna Karenina* by Clarence Brown, with Greta Garbo, and *Mutiny on The Bounty* by Frank Lloyd, with Clark Gable and Charles Laughton. In New York, where Fiorello La Guardia has been mayor for two years, on 10 October, there is the first night of *Porgy and Bess* by George Gershwin, at the Alvin Theatre.

It is in this same New York, and more precisely at Flatbush in Brooklyn, that Alan Stewart Konigsberg, destined to future fame under the name of Woody Allen, is born on 1st December. Unknown to him, events which will have a marked effect on his development are taking shape: Hitler, in power for two years in Germany, begins his anti-semitic persecution by depriving Jews of civil rights; Ingmar Bergman, seventeen years old, is studying at Uppsala, while Federico Fellini, fifteen, is lazily doing the same at Rimini; the Marx Brothers return to the cinema, going public with *A Night At The Opera*; Charlie Chaplin is putting the final touches to his most 'social' film, *Modern Times*.

What kind of childhood does a future genius of comedy have? Miserable and persecuted perhaps, like Charlie Chaplin in Kennington, South London, in poverty and neglect, or feeling lost and foreign, with the fresh memory of racial persecution, like the Marx Brothers on the Lower East Side of Manhattan. It has been said that comedy is bred by tragedy. Woody Allen's own childhood, if we listen to him, would seem to bear this out: forgetful, brutal parents, racist slurs, violent contemporaries. 'My parents were too poor to buy me a dog, so they got me an ant. I called him Spot.' 'I don't think my parents liked me. They put a live teddy bear in my crib.' 'I was kidnapped once. And my parents snapped into action immediately: they rented out my room.' 'My parents sent me to interfaith camp one summer. That meant I got beat up by kids of all faiths.'

These were some of the stories that the shy, young cabaret artist would tell as he clung to the microphone as if seeking support and encouragement, between stammers and 'ehmms' which seemed entirely natural. This was during the Sixties. Artists working in this field had had, until this time, the arrogant, confident manner of those who dominated the public. The newcomers regaled the audience with acerbic political observations, and used, without batting an eyelid, an abundance of four-letter words which no God-fearing citizen would have ever dreamt of using or expected to hear from other God-fearing citizens. Woody Allen and his misfortunes. . . . Maybe they weren't true, but they certainly resembled the truth. And the majority of his public accepted them at face value. So it was written, and word passed from mouth to mouth, about the modern rhapsody of the born loser and victim who, however, by laughing at himself, manages to make other people laugh, and so becomes a winner, thus conforming to the American fairy-tale of the self-made man.

But Mr Woody Allen and the comedian Woody were two completely different people. 'I really wasn't a scared and lonely child at all,' he himself declared during a frank interview in 1969. 'I played

Woody Allen, real name Alan Stewart Konigsberg, born at Flatbush (New York) on 1 December 1935, of a family of Jewish origin. His childhood, which was apparently normal and similar to that of his contemporaries, was to become not only a source of jokes for him but also of bleaker memories.

at all sorts of games and was good at quite a lot of them. I wasn't poor, or hungry or neglected. We were a well-fed middle-class family. We wore good clothes and lived in a comfortable house.'

Martin Konigsberg, Woody's father, was a goldsmith. During the economically uncertain period of the Thirties and Forties a major concern was to stay on one's feet, and so he even worked as a taxi driver, or a waiter at the Sammy Bowery Follies in Manhattan, where he was actually asked to perform music hall numbers from time to time. Woody's mother was Nettea (Nettie) Cherrie and she worked as a cashier in a Brooklyn flower shop. In 1943, Letty, his little sister, was born. She became the most precocious admirer of the budding young showman. All in all, he had a real family life.

Flatbush during the Thirties was not the same as the Lower East Side during the period from 1880–1910 when one and a half million poverty-ridden and illiterate Jews had moved in to escape the persecutions in Eastern Europe. The Marx Brothers were products of the Jewish ghetto which was not yet integrated into the melting pot of American society, and this was probably true also of Woody's grandparents, who came from Russia and Hungary. But Martin Konigsberg, born an American citizen in Brooklyn, and Nettea Cherrie, born an American citizen in the Lower East Side, did not belong to this group. Flatbush was a respectable area, not rich, but comfortable. It was populated by quiet, peaceable families from the lower middle class, who were concerned about economic security. It was a neighbourhood where people had certain values; as its famous citizen recalled later on in one of his most famous lines: 'They believed in God and carpeting.'

As a child, Woody showed no particular initiative. Neither a leader nor a rebel, his presence, even his very existence, seemed to pass unnoticed. All those who have diligently visited the ex-neighbours, ex-teachers and ex-schoolmates, in an attempt to reconstruct the formative years of the famous film artist, have found themselves faced with a complete blank wall.

His progress through public school N.99 and then Midwood High School was one of uninterrupted mediocrity. 'They were schools for emotionally disturbed teachers,' he was later to say. But he also admitted that he never did his homework, preferring to shut himself in his room, there to practise tirelessly conjuring and magic tricks. He read no books of any kind, only comics and the sport pages. His preferences were for basketball, boxing and, above all, baseball. He was crazy about Willie Mays ('the closest thing to a miracle or a magician'). He liked jazz. He loved the cinema. At every possible opportunity he would escape to go fishing or play in the open air. It would seem that despite the frail and sickly appearance, he was really a passable sportsman: as a young man he played 'second base' in the police baseball team, and he even tried boxing with some success.

What he did not like was socialising. He had very few friends, none of them close. He kept to himself. His schoolmates called him 'Red' because of his rust coloured hair: he didn't care for it, but he preferred to shut himself up in his shell rather than cause trouble. Later on, over the microphone, he would recount one of his fantasies on this matter. 'Floyd, the bully of the group, a vegetable mentality in a black leather jacket calls out, 'Hey, Red!' 'Red' is on his way to a violin lesson, and flares up. He puts down his instrument. 'My name is not Red. If you want me, call me by my regular name: Master . . . Heywood . . . Allen.' Pause. I spent that winter in a wheelchair, after a team of doctors had laboured to remove the violin. Lucky for me it wasn't a cello.'

An anonymous childhood and adolescence, it was not so very different from that of other children from the same social background in New York at that time. But in the memories (serious) of the adult Woody Allen, there is a continual dark note. 'I lacked for none of the creature comforts. But I was shy and everything dissatisfied me, although I don't know why.' Perhaps it was all a question of his character make up. After all, the film star, who is now rich, famous and sought after, spends his days hiding away, fleeing from his admirers and making such remarks as: 'Most of the time, I don't have

much fun. The rest of the time, I don't have any fun at all.' Or maybe it was something else.

In the America of the Nineteen Forties the air was alive with the myth of individual success and admiration for the he-man figure, who had courage, grit, and quick reflexes. And who pleased the girls. Someone who was small, with glasses and freckles on his face, could hardly fail to feel ugly and not on the same level as his fellows, and to regret (another famous line): 'not being someone else.'

However, as always in success stories of this type, there was a 'but.' The young man from Flatbush soon realised that he had one thing going for him. 'Even though I never laughed back then, I was still considered a funny boy. My point of view was funny, and I said funny things.'

So one fine day in 1952, Alan Stewart Konigsberg became Woody Allen. He had decided to become famous. He needed a stage name that had some of the allure of show business (and 'Woody Allen', in his opinion, had that allure) and a strategy. This strategy consisted of sending, by post, a series of funny stories to Walter Winchell and Earl Wilson whose names were the by-lines to the entertainment columns in the newspapers. These two needed jokes like a cook needs spices.

The results were encouraging and a number of his stories began to appear, and eventually his name actually appeared in print: Earl Wilson gave him credit for one of his jokes. 'Woody Allen says he ate in a restaurant with OPS prices: over people's salaries.' (explanatory note: OPS stood for Office of Price Stabilisation, the office of price controls).

This was not at a very high level, as he himself recognised later on, but it was the starting point for a continuous activity, a real profession. A public relations agency, David O. Alber Associates, who had among their clients famous people like Bob Hope, Guy Lombardo and Sammy Kaye, noticed his name in the paper and asked for a meeting. Woody arrived with his class books under his arm, and his jokes written out in a notebook. He was after all sixteen years old and had to go to school!

They reached the following agreement: fifty jokes a week, for twenty-five dollars. The agency then distributed the material to a dozen friendly columnists and they used the jokes, attributing them to one or other of the stars who were the agency's clients. This made the columns funny and kept the stars' names fresh in the public's consciousness.

Woody, at this point, felt himself to be 'at the very heart of show business.' Each day, when he had finished school, he took the subway to his employer's offices and jotted down fifty or so wisecracks. Many more than required, but how do you cool the ardour of youth?!

The youngster from Flatbush was thus launched on a type of work to be found, perhaps, only in the world of American entertainment and show business. He became a 'writer'; but it was often the case that this kind of writer did not actually write, but merely poured out a freewheeling series of jokes which an actor then refined before using them in the show.

At times, therefore, the writer was, in fact, a ghost-writer. He was the author of commissioned texts to which he had forfeited the rights and to which other people put their signatures. The areas he covered ranged from advertising to television, from cinema to theatre, and from variety to journalism. The more fortunate of these ghost-writers became credited script writers (their names appearing as authors of the text), or television producers, or comedy writers on Broadway. The majority continued to live anonymously, 'feeding the 'monster' according to their expression. The 'monster' could have been television, which insatiably devoured material, or even a single comedy actor. Bob Hope, it is said, eventually had a staff of a dozen writers, all tied to him on exclusive contracts.

This job for the agency, to be honest, was not really much to shout about. It was fine as a beginning, but it was not well paid (even if the wages did soon jump to forty-dollars a week) and, moreover, it did not offer any hope of advancement nor of a career. Allen's parents, for their part, turned up their noses at this nebulous occupation. For their son, they yearned for the security of a pharmacist, or better still, a doctor. However, in the end, once their son had promised not to abandon his studies, they gave in and introduced him to Abe Burrows, who was not only the comedy writer of *Guys and Dolls*, but also director, lyricist and script writer. Burrows enjoyed great respect and had a vast range of acquaintances in the world of entertainment and was a relative from Allen's mother's side of the family.

He met Woody, read his work, and was very encouraging: 'Don't worry. If you write jokes like these, you'll have no trouble.' He promised to do what he could and to show the material to the people who really counted. And since, in the meantime, the business of David O. Alber Associates began to suffer, it was at this point that things took the very turn that a script writer would have invented. One day an out of breath Woody arrived in the office. His immediate superior asked to see him at once. Before he had time to say 'good morning' his boss had handed him two weeks' wages and said: 'You're fired.' Woody put the money in his pocket and murmured: 'Oh, I . . . only came into the office to tell you I was leaving. NBC have offered me a job at 175 dollars a week.'

Something happened outside of work, as well. Woody Allen, under his real name of Alan Stewart Konigsberg, succeeded in getting his High School Certificate from Midwood High School, and had applied to and been accepted by New York University. It was an application made reluctantly, but the course was concerned with the world of entertainment, and, all in all, he had reason to hope that it wouldn't be too difficult: cinematographic production. The new student did not miss a single showing of the films which were the object of his studies (like a true fan), but on the other hand he missed almost all of the lessons. As a result, he found himself out after the first term. A little later, he tried again, taking evening classes at the City College of New York. The purpose, more than anything else, was 'in an effort to keep my mother from opening her wrists.' Here, too, things went badly. Scholastic studies were abandoned from then on, once and for all, but in curious contrast there now began the feverish reading of the self-taught. He did this because girls, about whom he had dreamt from the age of reason and even before, continually snubbed him. They had an exaggerated respect for education and only contempt for someone like him who had not got any. The feverish desire to catch up led him to read books. And from these banal motives, a genuine vocation was born.

But not all the girls were unfriendly. Harlene Rosen was tall, dark and good looking. At the age of fifteen she was probably the first representative of the female sex to pay any attention to Woody's advances. She studied hard, was developing a genuine interest in the arts and she played the piano very well. She represented both a stimulus and a support for him. She was calm where he was agitated: she was devoted to him and knew how to listen to him. It is reported that she did not have a very good sense of humour, and that she swallowed whatever he made up. But is this such a major defect? The two of them fell in love, or thought they did.

After working for several months in California for NBC, Woody couldn't stand the loneliness any more, and the idea of marriage began to seem like a way out of his situation. He phoned up Harlene on the other side of the Continent and asked her if she would marry him. He was nineteen, she was sixteen. She said 'yes'.

At the beginning of the Fifties, Hollywood was still the 'Mecca of the cinema,' the place where the majority of the world's inhabitants would have liked to live. What is more, it was also the capital of the growing television industry. For its script writers, the big screen dream factory often conjured up ugly nightmares and sleepless nights. The small screen dream factory made the same demands of its script writers, but without offering them any of the possible glory that was connected with film work. On the staff of the Writers' Development Program of the NBC, Woody Allen arrived in Hollywood to help prop up the *Colgate Comedy Hour*, a show

9

which was neither funny nor lighthearted, expect in intention. These were weeks of back-breaking work, during which he had no time to enjoy being in the presence of famous actors, well-known producers and mythical places. In fact, Hollywood and California turned out to be exactly the opposite to the tastes of the young scene writer from New York: too much sun, too superficial, too much emphasis placed on appearances. His life-long aversion to these things was born on this occasion.

But the trade had to be learnt in Hollywood. For Woody it was a revelation. The master who initiated Woody into the mysteries of his craft was Danny Simon, the brother of Neil Simon, who, some years later, was to become the most famous comedy writer in the United States. Danny Simon was an old hat at the gags and sketches. Woody was (in his own words) 'just some guy who knew how to make jokes.' Their meeting turned out to be fruitful: 'I've learned a couple of things on my own since, and modified things he taught me, but everything, unequivocally, that I learned about comedy writing I learned from him.'

The *Colgate Comedy Hour* went under anyway, in spite of the help given by Danny, Woody and all the other script writers involved. After months of Californian sunshine the long-awaited moment came to return to his native New York, with its terrible climate but stimulating people. Woody and Harlene had married (at the Hollywood Hawaiian Hotel), and, to return home, they now needed somewhere to live. They found a two-roomed apartment where they settled in without too many problems. She applied to Hunter College to study philosophy and Woody, at his typewriter, completed his transformation into a workaholic.

Television production was flowering in New York too. Woody wrote scripts for Buddy Hackett, Herb Shriner, Art Carney, Carol Channing, Kaye Ballard, Pat Boone, Jack Paar. And for Sid Caesar. In the Fifties, Sid Caesar was a living legend in television. He had made his mark from 1950 onwards with a show called *Your Show of Shows*, which lasted for more than nine years, changing name (first to *Caesar's Hour* and then to *Sid Caesar Invites You*), but not substance nor style. Brilliant, intelligent, excellently performed by the athletic and versatile comedian, this show boasted a staff of script writers and gagmen without equal. Half of the Broadway of the following decade, practically, worked on it. Neil Simon, Joseph Stein, Mike Stewart, Mel Brooks and Woody Allen himself. Plus Danny Simon, Larry Gelbart, Mel Tolkin, and Lucille Kallen. Although Woody worked in this hothouse, it seems that he didn't feel at home there. Only the chance of using a megaphone gave him some consolation! To understand why, it is sufficient to think of his character and then contrast it with a description of the work from another veteran of the staff, Albert Goldman: 'Every morning they all arrived, straight from their shrinks. They lit up their cigars and got into a circle around Sid, who recited, alone, the outlines of a sketch which had previously been prepared. As soon as he finished, everybody jumped up like a bunch of madmen. They screamed at each other and hurled jokes at each other, improvising bits of dialogue, until they

were tired out from laughing and sat down again. During all this chaos Sid had memorised sufficient material, and so he would start all over again with a new scene.'

Working for Caesar put a kind of seal of quality on Woody's rise, to the extent that in 1957 it even gained him the highly sought after Sylvania Award. This was the first of a long line of awards throughout his life for which he felt nothing but disdain. He was now lacking only one touch in his character formation, and this came with his experience in the 'Borscht Belt.' He obtained it in the summers, from 1956 to 1959. Borscht is a typical dish from Eastern Europe, and it proverbially symbolised the New York immigrant Jews, a bit like spaghetti for the Italians. Since the early decades of the century, on the mountains near New York, Poconos, Adirondack, Catskill, a series of small hotels sprang up. They were run by Jews and catered for a clientele of the same background. They became a chain of well-known tourist spots and came to be known as the 'Borscht Belt.' Besides the good food, the good climate and the sports facilities, they offered the added attraction of shows performed by rising young talents. Year after year 'the Belt' spawned comedians like Danny Kaye, Eddie Cantor, Jerry Lewis, Milton Berle, Sid Caesar, Buddy Hacket, Mel Brooks; and actors, writers, producers and directors.

Woody stayed at Camp Taminent. His task was simple in its mercilessness: every Saturday he had to go on with a new show, so he had seven days in which to write it, rehearse it and set it up. And it had to be of a very high standard. If there is any type of person with a very fine palate, when it comes to show business, then it is the New York Jew.

Everything went like clockwork. Woody wrote good scripts, full of gags, and what is more, for the first time he stepped away from the typewriter and assumed the role of producer, organising as many sketches for the other comedians as he did for himself. It was clearly an improvised production, but the result was far from poor. In the end, forced by the need to alternate with his colleagues, and encouraged by his familiarity with the holiday-making spectators, he even began to go on stage himself. His first efforts as an amateur performer were received only with indulgence, however. He was stiff, he fumbled his words, he was very shy and his voice could hardly be heard. Everyone, from the first to the last, advised him not to continue. At that point the future course of Allen's career could not possibly have been foreseen. In spite of all appearances, something was probably maturing inside him. Having reached the top in the activity he had chosen, he was now preparing for the leap into more difficult realms, following a characteristic that was to mark the various phases of his future work.

From 1958 Jack Rollins and Charles Joffe were Woody Allen's agents. Technically their job should have been limited to representing him, negotiating his contracts, finding work for him. And for this, they were to get 15 per cent of his earnings. In reality, their relationship went much deeper, based upon a loyalty of old-fashioned gentlemen (nothing written: the deal was clinched with a handshake and has survived right up to the present) and a protective, almost paternal devotion. Rollins and Joffe knew of their fledgling's feelings about the 'million comedians without credit' whom he saw being forced to sell his ideas. They listened to him reading aloud his sketches and gags, carrying himself just as a class comedian should. His material was autobiographic. Told by others, it had people in stitches. What then would happen if he himself started telling it? He had the physique for the task and the warmth of someone expressing something which is born from his own inventive powers. Also, being the agents of the author of funny stories meant getting 15 per cent of the author's fee for funny stories: being the agents of a star of a comedy show would mean a lot more.

So, in 1961, while he was working as a script writer for television's *Garry Moore Show*, Woody let himself be talked into making his debut as a performer. A small bar in Greenwich Village, the Duplex, agreed to try him out in their show. Free, and as a favour. It was a leap in the dark. Woody had stage fright: he was terrified by the public, and went through agony before going on stage. 'It was the worst year of my life. I'd feel this fear in my stomach every morning, the minute I woke up, and it would be there until I went on at 11 o'clock at night.' Nor was it a pleasant time for those around him. Charles Joffe himself confessed: 'Woody was just awful. Of course he had good lines. But he was so scared and embarrassed and – rabbity. If you gave him an excuse not to go on, he'd take it. Woody quit five or six times. We'd sit up all night talking him out of it.'

The show was not a success, but not just because of Woody's shyness. In the beginning, he was of the view that it was enough to tell good jokes, not realising that what was really important was the way in which he told them. Somebody who tries to hold the attention of an audience for three quarters of an hour by telling jokes that he does not know how to tell, is merely an irritating windbag. All the same, he kept on trying. He gained confidence in front of an audience, and he grew used to making a burlesque parody of his own awkwardness, and, little by little, he defined the outline of his surreal-istic anti-hero for whom everything always went wrong. Terrified or not, he made the audience laugh. 'The jokes become a vehicle for the person to display a personality or an attitude, just like Bob Hope. . . . You're laughing at character all the time. . . . What I'm really interested in, is creating an image of a warm person that people will accept as funny apart from the joke.'

Having had his apprenticeship, he did not have to wait long to perform at a venue of greater prestige and elegance. The Blue Angel was 'uptown', meaning outside the boundaries of the republic of students and intellectuals which made up the Village. It paid accordingly. Since Garry Moore had sacked him from his show and his weekly income had fallen from 1700 dollars to a few pennies, it seemed like the right solution at the right time.

In November 1962, he returned to Greenwich Village, but he was not just retracing his footsteps. At the Bitter End he was greeted with a regular contract and a warm welcome from the public (he recalls it as 'a great uproar'). In the *New York Times* of 21 November 1962, the critic Arthur Gelb recommended the show 'to whoever wants to see a young comedian promising to become an estab-lished young comedian.' From then on, having made a name for himself, the life of the young comedian became a rapid merry-go-round of venues and per-formances: at Mister Kelly's in Chicago; at the Crystal Palace in Saint Louis; at the hungry i (all in small letters: the i stands for intellectual) in San Francisco; at the Crescendo in Los Angeles; at Shadows in Washington; and a very large number of venues in New York. Added to this merry-go-round were his appearances as a guest on television variety shows, concerts for university students, and even the issue of three LPs bearing his name and featuring his monologues.

During the early decades of the century, comedians plied their trade on the vaudeville stages, where they learnt how to be part mime artist and part clown, part singer and part dancer. After the Second World War, the scene moved to the night clubs. These little establishments had mushroomed to the extent that a comedian could change club every night, and work all year, without even leaving Brooklyn.

Young men like Lenny Bruce or veterans like Henny Youngman went out under the lights, took up the microphone and talked, trying to make the audience laugh. They were defined as Stand-up Comedians, standing alone before the audience.

From the point of view of the classical showman, their shows were almost sacrilege, because they excluded the element of mime as a way of making people laugh. Most of these shows were of very poor quality. Stan Laurel had a very biting opinion to express about them: 'They're all the same, or almost all. The same dark blue suits, the same tired jokes about their wives: how thin they are, how fat they are, how stingy they are. I only hope that they really do have the type of wife that they describe.'

But the public had changed. By 1950 the number of people holding degrees in America had doubled compared to ten years earlier. The university population was on the increase and destined to reach, by 1968, a total of six million, four times the number of 1940. The public had clearly defined tastes in matters of music, literature, cinema, strip cartoons. And in what made them laugh. Subtle humour with words and intellectual acrobatics were much more acceptable than knock-out comedy. Mort Sahl was the new hero. This was in 1954. He would come onto the stage in a very different way from his older colleagues in their blue suits: a pullover and an open-necked shirt, a daily paper under his arm. He would sit down, open the paper and begin: 'I see here in the paper. . . .' No jokes about the wife: instead he attacked Eisenhower, Nixon, McCarthy, Foster Dulles. Some time later, Dick Gregory amazed a white public by addressing them on equal terms, even though he was black; and Dick Davy, a Jew, delighted a black audience by haranguing them about racism.

These were followed by Mike Nichols and Elaine May, the Second City Group, Bernie Travis, Robert Klein, Bill Cosby, Dick Cavett, all intellectual comedians who took their material from culture and politics and had little in common with the light-hearted chatter of their pre-war colleagues.

Even the newly arrived Woody Allen was labelled 'cerebral', 'intellectual.' In actual fact his subject matter was much less intellectual than that of many others. It was taken from his private life, autobiographic.

His marriage to Harlene had deteriorated to the point that it ended in divorce: this led him to open the floodgates to a series of gags about his ex-wife. It was the start of a course of psychoanalytic therapy that has never been discontinued. Freud and Jung became subject matter for jokes. He had a frustrated childhood and adolescence. He turned derision into his battle-horse. Nevertheless he still expressed himself in a somewhat vague manner. He started off like a lecturer ('I think I will review for you some of the outstanding features of my private life and put them into perspective. Then we'll have a brief question-and-answer period and evaluate them.') and,

through mental acrobatics, he wound his way onwards. He loved paradox ('I don't know if you can see this, but it's a very handsome watch. My grandfather, on his death-bed, sold me this watch.') and made frequent use of anticlimax (Not only is God dead, but try getting a plumber on weekends.') and even the absurd ('I went to NYU myself. I was a philo major there. I was thrown out of NYU in my freshman year. I cheated on my Metaphysics Final. I looked within the soul of the boy sitting next to me.'). The intellectuals, writers and journalists adopted him as their darling. After all, he was one of them, a writer, and they shared his sense of humour. In order to remain faithful to this side of his nature, Woody took great care not to give up writing. On the contrary, he aimed even higher. He began to publish notes and funny stories in the aristocratic *New Yorker*, and then in other magazines. In later years, there were even people who spoke of him as one of the greatest American comic writers.

One evening in 1964, at the Blue Angel, while watching Woody Allen's show, Shirley MacLaine laughed till she cried. Sitting next to her, Charles K. Feldman, the film producer who had accompanied her, began chewing over some ideas involving this strange comedian. The next day he sent a messenger to Rollins and Joffe: would their protegé like to write the screenplay for a film? Certainly, they said, for 35,000 dollars and a part in the film. Feldman, who would have been willing to pay double, hastily concluded an agreement. The film was to be called *What's New, Pussycat?* and was to be about an incorrigible womaniser and his sincere but hopeless efforts to convert to monogamy. It was intended to be very funny, full of beautiful, voluptuous women, with a modern setting, and many references to psychoanalysis. For a production of this kind, Woody Allen seemed to have fallen like manna from heaven, and Feldman, who had a great nose for talent, had no hesitation in backing him, in spite of Woody's complete lack of experience. But that was his style: from the various branches of show business he recruited a number of other skilled collaborators who were also to become better known in the

world of films. Amongst them were the director Clive Donner, and the composer Burt Bacharach.

Originally, *What's New, Pussycat?* was supposed to be in black and white, with a small budget. Instead, as often happens in the film industry, it turned out to be completely different. The cast mushroomed until it included Peter Sellers, Ursula Andress, Capucine, Romy Schneider, Paula Prentiss; the film was made in colour; the star was Peter O'Toole, fresh from the award-winning film *Lawrence of Arabia* (in place of the original candidate, Warren Beatty).

The filming took place in London and Paris throughout 1964, and it was finally presented to the public in June 1965. It was a sensation. The crowds flooded the cinemas, and very quickly *What's New, Pussycat?* broke all records for box-office takings for comedy films.

By far the least famous name among the star-studded cast, Woody Allen, who was also the script writer, found he had become a celebrity overnight. The doors to the world of the cinema, to which he had secretly aspired, were now open to him. Surprisingly, his reaction was one of fury. '*Pussycat* was such an unpleasant experience for me. . . . The people in charge just killed it completely. I fought

with everybody all the time. I hated everyone, and everyone hated me.' 'They wanted a girl-girl sex-sex picture to make a fortune. I had something else in mind. They got a girl-girl sex-sex picture which made a fortune.' 'A lot of ad-libbing went on, which I like in the films I direct, but there was nobody on *Pussycat* to control the ad-libbing. Consequently it could be very funny, but sometimes it wasn't. But there was nobody in charge who knew how to winnow out the good stuff from the bad. They just slopped it all up on the screen.' Woody got to the stage of complaining in public about not being able to take legal action against anyone for what had been done to him.

What's New Pussycat? certainly wasn't a masterpiece. It was a huge show business spectacular, aiming at mass market success. But within these limits it was not at all bad: it had good music, was well acted, kept up a fair pace, and overflowed with its own lively and intelligent humour. It was chaotic and uneven, but it had that touch of zaniness that set it apart from the run-of-the-mill comedy films of those days. The contempt for it, that Woody displayed over and over again, was really contempt for a certain type of cinema.

Charles K. Feldman was one of Hollywood's last

tycoons. He had presided over the careers of some of the brightest stars, from Clark Gable to Marilyn Monroe.

He spent vast sums of money in his quest for the super production at any price. He squandered enormous amounts on sudden changes of mind, perhaps moving a film, which had already been set up, from Rome to Paris. Anybody working on the film was an employee, who had to obey him and whose work could be manipulated at any time and in any way. They called him 'The Caliph' or 'King Midas.' He had the arrogance of a king, and also the sudden bursts of generosity.

All this was at loggerheads with Woody Allen's ideas. He was used to writing and telling his own stories, or publishing them without any cuts; he thought of himself as an author. He rejected the star system, production line methods, inefficiency and everything 'mammoth', but most of all he denied anybody the right to touch his work once it seemed satisfactory to him. He made a promise, to himself and to others: 'I decided I would never do another film unless I had complete control of it.'

This resolution was of short duration. Charles K. Feldman was not at all worried by his young recruit's cutting remarks. He decided that the contract he was holding, which anticipated more films, was worth enforcing. His new project for 1966 was entitled *Casino Royale*. Of all the books written by Ian Fleming about the secret agent James Bond, only one had not been bought by the producer Albert R. Broccoli to make into a film: this was *Casino Royale*. This one belonged to Feldman. However, it was impossible to think of making it into a 'serious film': the actor Sean Connery was tied to Broccoli and the public just would not accept another James Bond. So they thought of an 007 in *Pussycat* style: chaotic, crazy, and comic. The plot was completely rewritten, way beyond the limits of probability. The 'real' 007 is David Niven, recalled to the service after some years in retirement. Mata Bond, the daughter of 007 and Mata Hari, is involved. The head of the abominable secret organisation pitted against the counter-espionage service is ex-secret agent Bond's idiot nephew, Woody Allen himself.

Woody accepted the role. All he was asked to do was act. ('I didn't have to write anything. I could just go over there and hope that it would turn out to be a good film.') His participation was put on the same level as that of celebrities like David Niven, Peter Sellers, Ursula Andress, Orson Welles, and 'at that time in my career any job in movies was better than no job.' It was a fair compromise then. But in spite of the film's success, and in spite of the additional popularity that went with it, in spite of the handsome cheque handed to him by the producer, Woody once again reacted furiously. 'I sat around in London for about five and a half months on salary waiting to shoot. They shot me for five or six days and that was it. I never bothered to see the film. I knew it would be a horrible film from what was going on there. It was a chaotic madhouse. I knew then that the only way to make films is to control it completely.'

However, the run-up to the start of Woody Allen's career as a film director did not end here. During 1966, there was a third episode. 'A man whom I eventually wound up sueing, and winning – I always wind up sueing – asked me if I'd look at a Japanese film he had bought. He didn't know what to do with the thing. I saw it, and thought it might be a funny idea to put a different story in their mouths.' The film was a shoddy series product inspired by the James Bond trend, and it was originally called *The Key of The Keys*. In the rewritten version it was entitled *What's Up, Tiger Lily?* It told the story of two rival Japanese gangs who spoke like Brooklyn Jews. Called Phil Moskowitz, in spite of his appearance, the hero's ambition is to acquire a special recipe for hard boiled egg salad, 'because it is written that he who has the best recipe for egg salad will rule over the Heavens and the Earth.' Woody also added some inserts to the original film, giving himself and some of his friends the chance to amuse themselves with their usual word games. 'Then the producer changed a couple of lines in it and I sued him (for the record, the producer was a certain

Henry Saperstein). Against all the odds, the film was a great success. Woody commented acidly; 'It was done at such a low price, and the idea was so novel that it was almost hard for them not to make money with it.'

1966 was a crucial year. Apart from the two film experiences, it brought two other changes: a second marriage and a debut on Broadway.

His wedding with Louise Lasser took place on 2nd February. The new Mrs Allen was an actress and a singer: she had worked in the theatre in the same company as Barbra Streisand (she had even been her understudy), she had appeared frequently on television and in a scene from *What's New, Pussycat?* (she massaged the shoulders of the psychoanalyst, Peter Sellers, during the group therapy session). She was the daughter of the famous tax expert, S. Jay Lasser, and a certain cynic immediately remarked that such a union was to be expected between a tax specialist and a man who was now earning more than 250,000 dollars a year. The couple had met in 1961. 'When we first met,' she later remembered, 'we would go for long walks in the park, and talk about art and philosophy and life, and all those things you find out months later that neither of you likes to do.' The scene could have been taken from one of Woody's films.

In the end, his marriage with Louise was no more fortunate than the one with Harlene. Their divorce was finalised in 1969. They remained, however, very good friends, and the cheerful, red-headed actress later filled major roles in several films directed by her ex-husband.

The new matrimonial home, in keeping with their new economic circumstances, was very different from the badly furnished few square metres of his previous apartment. This time it was a badly furnished apartment of a great many square metres. It contained a juke-box which did not work, a billiard table which no-one used, small spotlights designed to illuminate newly purchased paintings (which were piled up somewhere awaiting the time when their owner would decide where to hang them; and there they remained). Some years later they added a terrace which was faithfully maintained in the style of a Japanese garden, with rubber snakes to frighten the pigeons which defecated everywhere. The pigeons, of course, were not frightened in the least, but one rubber snake fell on a lady who sued as a result.

In the autumn, public performances began of *Don't Drink The Water*, the work which marked Woody Allen's move from cabaret to 'legitimate' theatre. It was a play in two acts, not particularly original and fairly static, but it was enlivened by some touches of clever satire and an absolute

17

barrage of jokes. The story concerned a small-town family from New Jersey who, while on holiday, end up by accident in an Iron-curtain country and are mistaken for spies. Complicating matters still further is the idiot son of the local American ambassador.

During rehearsals of the play there were endless problems, from casting changes to continual alterations to the script. Half way through the practice tour (it is normal for American companies to polish their shows in the provinces before confronting the hyper-critical New York audience) the director himself, Bob Sinclair, was sacked and the possibility was seriously discussed of giving up the idea of Broadway and just doing a couple of performances in Florida. In the end, however, everything was sorted out and the show 'Opened' on 17th November 1966, under the direction of Stanley Prager and with Lou Jacobi in the principal role. Woody did not take part and lived the theatrical experience only as the playwright, supervising the performance of his work.

Takings were good at the box-office: the show ran for almost two years. Less warm was the reception from the critics. 'Allen has written jokes, jokes, nothing but jokes,' complained the theatre critic of the *New York Times*, Walter Kerr. 'The comic inventions become more and more irritating as the action proceeds, for the simple reason that there is nothing of substance to support them. I do not know if anyone has ever said that one comic situation is better than a thousand puns; if no-one has ever said it, then now is the time.' The debutant dramatist, with characteristic dissatisfaction, recognised the structural defects in his work and the lack of substance in its plot. He justified himself by saying to people that his sole aim had been to write an out-and-out box-office success. What he did not say, but which everyone recognised, was that at just thirty-one years of age he had achieved another of the major goals in his career.

Divorced for the second time, Woody now found himself once more leading the bachelor life. He had nothing against girls, on the contrary; according to one of his best friends, the actor Tony Roberts, he was almost in the same clan as the ever-eager Harpo Marx when it came to skirt-chasing. However, his awkward temperament made him ill at ease. His friends tried their best to introduce him to suitable candidates for a place in his heart, but Woody either remained silent or put on false airs and poses. He realised that, strangely enough, he could only relax completely with one type of woman: those towards whom he had no thoughts of conquest, the wives of his good friends. This led him to think of the dilemma in which he would be placed if one of them was to fall in love with him. Without having had the experience in real life, he decided to use it as a plot for a comedy and wrote *Play It Again, Sam*.

The story concerns Allan Felix, a film critic, totally besotted with his idol Humphrey Bogart, but completely inept in real life. His wife leaves him, he wallows in despair, his friends try to find him someone new, and, after a number of misadventures, he ends up falling in love with Linda, who is his best friend's wife. Rather than cause them problems, he decides to make a 'Bogart-like' sacrifice and draws back. All ends well: a young cinema student discovers that he is the famous cinema critic she admired so much while working on her thesis, and . . . the implication is that they will have a long and happy life together.

The play went on stage in New York on 12th February 1969. The cast included Woody Allen, his first experience as a real theatrical actor, Tony Roberts, Diane Keaton and Jerry Lacey. The play was also the debut for the director, Joseph Hardy. It was Allen's second attempt on Broadway as a comic playwright and this time the critics acclaimed it. In the influential *New York Times*, Clive Barnes wrote in his article, 'Woody Allen is anything but a simple gagman: on the contrary he is a theatrical talent who should do much better, and he probably will.'

Allen also received unanimous praise for his own acting, which was what he had always considered his weak point. He certainly still wasn't (and perhaps was never to become) an actor in the classical sense of the word, but the years in night

clubs had given him a greater mastery of himself on the stage. Moreover, in this instance he had the advantage of portraying his own character. Underneath it all, Allan Felix 'was' Woody Allen.

The show ran for 453 performances and was one of the hits of that time. Acting on stage became a pleasure for Woody. 'To go over to a theatre at eight o'clock at night, and do a show, and get big laughs for an hour and a half, and that is all you have worked for the day, then you're finished, is very gratifying.'

There was something else that he enjoyed as well. Diane Keaton had come into his life. Into his theatrical life at first: when the auditions were being held for the show, this Californian girl, who was playing a small part in *Hair*, created the impression that the role of Linda had been written just for her. At the same time, she entered Allen's private life with an intensity and depth greater than anyone who had preceeded her.

Woody found someone who was both sensitive and spontaneous, yet insecure and shy (*Hair* was famous as a musical because those participating performed in the nude: only one actress remained clothed and she was Diane Keaton); a personality who brought vitality and freshness to Woody, allowing him not only to be himself, but also to act a guide and a mentor. This relationship, which never evolved into marriage, lasted for almost two years, and then continued almost unaltered in the form of a close friendship. At least, until the meeting with Mia Farrow, this was the most important personal experience in the life of Woody Allen.

The principal event of 1969 was, however, the release of *Take The Money And Run*, the first film written, directed and acted by Woody. It was the realisation of a dream: he had total control over the work, a control which, in the entire history of American film-making, had been given to almost no-one else (far less somebody making their first film). The executive producer was Charles Joffe himself, Woody's manager. As far as Palomar Pictures was concerned, the small and recently formed production house which invested one and a

half million dollars, it was a big risk, even though it was a calculated one. 'I had some moderate record in this sense,' explained Woody. 'I had written a play for Broadway that worked. I had written the script to *What's New, Pussycat?* which made a lot of money even though I hated it, and I was a comedian and a writer so I was a reasonable choice. I mean, they felt it was not just a complete crazy. . . . The major companies probably wouldn't have taken a chance with me. But Palomar couldn't go to the great directors and make deals so quickly, so they were willing to take a chance on me for a moderate price, I mean, for the film a moderate price.'

The film opened in New York on 19th August 1969. Despite complaining of a certain monotony, the *New York Times* critic, Vincent Canby, praised this first attempt ('Allen is, in the strict sense, a beginner; but the film represents the almost perfect cinematographic equivalent to his best night club monologues') and appreciated in particular Allen's ability to create visual comedy of the same high quality as the verbal comedy.

At that time, the American public was in the grip of a wave of nostalgia; nostalgia for the days before Vietnam, the 'clean' years of the Twenties and Thirties. In a period of crisis of national identity, many people looked to the cinema as the mirror in which that national identity was reflected and celebrated without scepticism.

Traditional Hollywood was dying and directors were emerging who had been brought up with the cinema, worshipping it from childhood: Bogdanovich, Scorsese, Lucas, Spielberg. They used the cinema of the past and incorporated it into their 'new' cinema; distorting it, quoting it, parodying it, reforming it. And alongside this new group, the new film-maker now took his place. He was comic and disrespectful like Groucho Marx, bespectacled like Harold Lloyd, like Buster Keaton he was impassive in the face of life's vicissitudes. A renovator, Woody was also an innovator, with much that was his own and original. People made comparisons, especially between Allen and that other great proponent of the comedy of the absurd, Groucho Marx. Groucho himself made his feelings known. 'They say Allen got something from the Marx Brothers. He didn't. He is an original. The best. The funniest.'

Even so, Allen's first attempt had not gone smoothly. He had shot reels of film and had then not been able to assemble it. He had encountered two major problems: firstly, the plot was so weak as to be almost non-existent; then there was the temptation to insert dramatic scenes, the forerunners of the 'major' themes that he would deal with at much greater length when he reached maturity as a director. Different versions of the film were prepared, and on various occasions they were shown to selected audiences. Each time the result was disappointing. When everything seemed totally lost, things finally started to go better when Ralph Rosenblum, an experienced film editor, was called in to help. He was a man who did not mince his words. Perhaps because of their contrasting characters, Woody hit it off with him at once. Rosenblum threw out the dramatic scenes, re-inserted other good sequences which had been discarded, and made critical changes to the soundtrack (particularly in the music). Most significantly, he advised Woody to shoot a new ending, strong enough to tie up the plot of the film. The young director followed his advice. Rosenblum was the first of a string of top-class professionals who, little by little, gathered around Woody and ended up by becoming the backbone of his team. The lesson about the new ending was not lost: from that time on, Woody never started a camera rolling without first including days or weeks in the work schedule for further takes, to correct, to remake and to perfect; and, in particular, to work over the final scenes, a curious weakness in his script writing talent.

Bananas was his second work. Stylistically, it was closely related to the previous one and even to *What's New, Pussycat?*: it was what its author defined as 'formless comedy', i.e. a comic spectacle with no rigid structure. Effectively, it was the simple outline of a story, onto which all the nonsensical ideas were heaped.

It was premiered in New York on 28th April 1971, and it was acclaimed. Vincent Canby, the *New York Times* critic, defined it as 'scandalously funny.' The public flooded the cinemas. It was a success; but not a great success, just like all the subsequent films that were to be Woody Allen's alone. Worshipped by a discriminating audience, mainly in the big cities, Woody has never penetrated the mass market and has always been content with modest ventures.

Above all, it was United Artists who showed the most magnaminity. Woody worked with them until 1980, on almost unbelievable contractual conditions, which gave him all the advantages, including total creative control. Yet United Artists were never repaid with massive box-office receipts.

Also in 1971, *Getting Even* appeared in the bookshops. It was a collection of his best humourous pieces, which had appeared in various magazines. It was about this time (a bit too early, to be entirely truthful) that students began to write their degree theses on the subject of Woody Allen: 'Everybody writes their thesis on Bergman,' he commented sardonically, 'but children prefer something amusing when they are doing their homework.'

The year ended on a bitter note. In December, the *Woody Allen Comedy Special* was filmed, the title being later changed to *The Politics of Woody Allen*. It was his only explicit work of political satire, and it was also the only work of his which was censored.

The work had been commissioned by the PBS (Public Broadcasting Service), a public network and therefore a dwarf among the private giants of the American television industry. Woody was in favour of public initiatives and he appreciated the freedom from commercial pressures that it offered. For a nominal fee, he accepted the opportunity of writing, directing and acting in the *Special*, and decided to use it to get at the Nixon presidency.

The short, half-hour film was never broadcast. Various excuses were made, but it was soon clear that the real reason was the veto placed on it by the White House.

Woody mixed up documentary film from the archives with new scenes, to tell the story of Harvey

Wallinger (Henry Kissinger, obviously), played by himself. 'If you want something done, you have to be in good with Harvey. If Mrs Nixon wants to kiss her husband, she has to kiss Harvey first.' 'Attorney-General John Mitchell has many ideas for strengthening the country's law-enforcement methods and is hampered only by lack of funds and the Constitution.'

The other jokes are more inoffensive (and less funny) than these, demonstrating Woody's basic unfamiliarity with the very idea of political satire. Nixon, however, came under fire again later on. 'The greatest comedian in the world?' commented Woody to a journalist in 1974. 'Why, Richard Nixon, of course. He's been playing Watergate for two years now, and the show still has half the world laughing.'

In 1969, Howard Morris, an actor from Sid Caesar's old team, brought *Don't Drink The Water* to the screen. Woody played no part in it and was completely disinterested in the venture. In fact, he even complained: 'Once I write the thing, and it opens, they can treat me like a dead author. I sold *Don't Drink The Water* to films, and I couldn't care less if they made it into a musical, or made it into a terrible movie, which they did.'

On the other hand, he became actively involved in the screen version of *Play It Again, Sam*, although without much enthusiasm. He accepted the offer from Paramount (which had made sure of the rights a long time in advance) to be both script writer and actor, because for him 'acting in films was a creative job' and compensated for the trouble involved in writing screen-plays, which was 'not at all a creative job'. Practically the whole company which had worked on the stage was present on the set. The director was Herbert Ross, who was already well-known for *Goodbye Mr Chips* and for *The Owl And The Pussycat*.

Everything went well right from the start. The film sequences were shot without any problems. Ross, who had already won Woody's goodwill at the script writing stage ('It took me about ten days to do. It was so easy to do. . . . And Herb had some

very good suggestions for the screenplay'), kept to the work plan, he kept to the predicted budget and he kept things under tight control, showing that he knew what he wanted. The editing of the film was fast and efficient, and the previews were a success. On the 4th May 1972 the film was ready to receive the applause of Allen's New York supporters. It went very well. It had been changed from the original play just enough to make it new without making it too different. Instead of New York, it was set in San Francisco, it had a sweet and sour ending instead of a happy one, and it allowed a lot of scope to Diane Keaton in her role. For the twenty-six year old actress (no relation of Buster Keaton, although she had a cat called Buster) the film was effectively her debut on the screen. 1972 was also the year that *The Godfather* came out, in which she played the minor part of the wife of Michael Corleone-Al Pacino.

Three months passed, and in the middle of the New York summer along came Woody Allen again with a film he had made between the takes of *Play It Again, Sam*, and which had a place much closer to his heart: *Everything You Always Wanted To Know About Sex*, written, directed and interpreted by him. It was in a number of episodes and the title (but only the title) came from a popular sex manual which had achieved great success in the United States.

This time, critical opinions were divided. On the one side was the majority of his indulgent supporters, led by Vincent Canby ('The film is fragmentary, but if you are fans of Allen, like I am, that makes no difference'); and from the other side came the attacks of the more critical viewers who counted the episodes and noted that, out of seven, one at the most stood out. The public was with the indulgent critics, and the box-office takings were good this time as well.

In this way, at the cost of perhaps half a false step, Woody concluded his apprenticeship. Although inexperienced, he emerged unscathed from the three films made against contemporary trends, and now had every right to call himself a film director. As the self-taught person that he was, he had learned the

Woody Allen and Andrea Marcovicci in a scene from
Martin Ritt's *The Front*. Having spent years making
his audience laugh, Allen here tackles his first dramatic
role.

trade by playing the trade. He enjoyed a great deal
of favour from many critics, people tended to
protect the flower of his talent from the pain of
disapproval and show respect for him. At the
opening of his film on sex, the New York press,
openly complicit, published a light-hearted interview with him on the same subject. He was beginning to be discovered by the Europeans, little by
little taking over from the now played out Jerry
Lewis.

His ambitions grew. The idea of 'formless

comedy' vanished from his mind, just like the
comics of chaos, like the Marx brothers, ceased to
exercise their influence on him. Anyone asking him
the names of the film-makers he preferred the most,
were now told: Ingmar Bergman, Federico Fellini,
Michelangelo Antonioni. His next films *Sleeper*
(1973) and *Love And Death* (1975) were still very
funny, but they had a better crafted and more
'classical' structure. Both films, especially *Love And
Death*, contained more serious themes, 'messages'
more or less openly addressed to the public.

23

Woody Allen and Michael Murphy in *The Front*, a film
which recalls the 'witch-hunts' led by Senator Joseph
McCarthy in the early Fifties.

In 1977, with the launch of the comic strip *Inside
Woody Allen*, the break with the past became final.
Woody the clown, Woody the caricature, now only
existed in the cartoons (at first by Joe Marthen and
then by Stuart Hample). As author, Woody Allen
confined himself to a kind of distracted supervision.

In the large attic overlooking Central Park, where
Woody had moved at the time of his second
marriage, the decorating had finally been completed, with taste and sobriety. Perhaps the only eccentric touch was the huge canopied bed which
appeared out of proportion for its function as a
place for sleeping, or even for loving. In fact, it was

the holy of holies: Woody didn't do his writing in
an office, but in bed. The rest of the house was
overflowing with books and records. The world of
culture had become the world of Woody Allen,
something which could be discovered by any reader
of his humorous essays and any attentive spectator
at his films. Literature and philosophy (especially
European) had become subjects to quote and
parody. With them as the 'bricks' he constructed his
creative edifice and he regarded them as qualitative
targets at which to aim.

They were also something more: they demon-
strated the importance of the creator's point of

view. Just like the great intellects he admired, Woody was defining his lines of enquiry. Each new film was to be an attempt at a new direction, a sign of development and a challenge to his own talent.

Instead of the easy repetition of a successful formula, which would have brought him wealth and fame, he preferred the risk of total failure and laying himself open to accusations of presumption.

His moral sense became stronger as well. For years he had stated that his only ambition was to have his audience in stitches, but now he took up more mature attitudes towards the themes of human behaviour, both in society and in private.

It was in this spirit that he decided to participate as an actor in *The Front* (1976), which was about the years of the 'witch hunts'. He found himself out of place in a dramatic role, and the film, tamely directed by Martin Ritt, was not worthy of him. But, 'the subject was worth it', he said. 'Martin and the script writer Walter Bernstein have actually lived through the black-list period, and they emerged with dignity.' (We should bear in mind that the actors and intellectuals, accused of Communist sympathies, whose names appeared on the list were effectively barred from working.)

Annie Hall (1977) was the first work of the 'new' Woody Allen, and it was a memorable achievement. While the audience laughed at the jokes, at the same time they were moved by the human dilemmas of Alvy and Annie, treated in the film with restraint and sensitivity. Comparisons began to be made openly between the work of the director from Flatbush and that of Ingmar Bergman. In April 1978, against all expectations, *Annie Hall* won a number of Oscars: best picture, best director, best screenplay, best actress (Diane Keaton). Woody stayed well away from the mad Hollywood scene and did not collect the statuettes. With his typical scorn for this type of recognition, he refused to allow any mention of the awards to appear in the advertising for the film. And if anyone expected him to cash in on his success, they were to be proved wrong once again. Having received the seal of popular acclaim with the Oscars, Woody made a heavy intellectual,

elitist film, *Interiors*, in which he did not even appear. There was nothing light-hearted about it, only an atmosphere reminiscent of Bergman or Chekhov. Was this the end of Woody Allen the comedian? Almost before his fans had the time to ask this question, another film was released, *Manhattan*. It was judged to be (and maybe it is) his masterpiece. That was how it was described by Richard Schickel in *Time* (30th April 1979), adding that it was a 'perfect blend of style and content, of humour and humanity.' '*Manhattan* is his most moving and expansive work to date,' praised the ever loyal Vincent Canby in the *New York Times*. With his ninth work, Woody Allen had reached the top. From both sides of the Atlantic the praise poured in, and very few now doubted that he belonged to the ranks of top class film-makers, the ones who leave a lasting impression.

But the enthusiasm received a set-back with his 1980 film, *Stardust Memories*. Having found his own original style in *Manhattan*, Woody began imitating others again: this time it was Federico Fellini. The lightness of touch was gone, and in its place could be detected a dark misanthropy. Some of his most committed supporters did an about-face. Pauline Kael, doyenne of the New York film critics, wrote dryly: 'To say this picture is not funny is putting it mildly; it is not good either.' The chorus of criticism grew in volume when the time came, on 27th April 1981, for the reviewers to see his new stage play, *The Floating Lightbulb*, at the Vivan Beaumont Theatre in New York. The few kind words said about it were for the actors and the director, Ulu Grosbard. This comedy-drama was judged to be weak and badly constructed. *Variety* lamented the obvious influence of Tennesse Williams, Clifford Odets and Arthur Miller. Clive Barnes, from the columns of the *New York Post*, spoke of a confused beginning, of a plot full of clichés and insufficient care taken with the dramatic effects; Walter Kerr, in the *New York Times*, wrote, 'It is all so arbitrary: failure has been forced . . . by Mr Allen, perhaps so that even in Brooklyn they will seem more like Chekhov.'

The third phase in Woody's plunging descent was the arrival of *A Midsummer Night's Sex Comedy*, in July 1982. It was a simple lighthearted film: so lighthearted that it, appeared vacuous. Could Andrew Sarris, another mandarin among New York Critics, have been right when he wrote nine years earlier that Allen had been over-rated to the detriment of a large number of other film-makers, much more professional than him?

In addition to his lack of artistic success, there was Woody's not overly endearing personal behaviour. Apart from a very restricted circle of friends (Louis Lasser, Diane Keaton, the actors Tony Roberts and Michael Murphy, the script writer Marshall Brickman, the television producer Jean Doumanian), Woody was inaccessible.

Between his admirers, journalists, all his collaborators, and himself, he interposed a wall of indifference and annoyance. Usually self-controlled and well-mannered, sometimes he let himself go in angry or arrogant scenes, like the time that he shouted at his set designer who, because his leg was in plaster, had made Woody lose a few seconds getting into the car.

To many people he also seemed to be a hypocrite. 'I never read the critics,' he boasted; but he often saw the most important critics and sent them complimentary letters about their articles. 'I have very frugal tastes and needs,' he added, and then he was seen being taken around in a chauffeur driven Rolls-Royce, no less. 'I am happy in my shell,' he concluded; but almost every evening he could be found with his group and with Mia Farrow, his new lady friend, at Elaine's Restaurant, the latest 'in' place, frequented by the city's celebrities. People also began to find certain characteristics irritating, while before they had seemed eccentric, like his habit of always dressing casually. At the beginning of his relationship with Louise Lasser, he had made an enemy of the hall porter at her apartment block who, seeing him so badly dressed, had insisted that he use the service entrance on more than one occasion. In theory, he dressed casually to render himself unrecognisable to autograph hunters, but Diane Keaton, with typical candour, had not failed to point out that, camouflaged in an old hat and dark glasses, he attracted attention anyway: in an old hat and dark glasses he looked like Peter Sellers! In any case, his jeans, shirts and shapeless jackets were all made to measure by a well-known tailor. Last of all, there was this business of jazz. Since the beginning of the Seventies, Woody had been in the habit of playing the clarinet in an amateur group, every Monday evening, in a place called *Michael's Pub*. According to many connoisseurs his performances, in the pure New Orleans style, were far from bad. But he never smiled, he never looked at the audience, and at the end he left hastily without a word. What was this behaviour all about? Was it natural reserve, or was it not rather a sign of outright snobbery.

At last *Zelig* came along. Peace was made with everyone. Seemingly haphazard in its construction, but in reality intricate and intelligent, this highly elaborate film satisfied both the connoisseur and the laymen. Woody, along with his director of photography Gordon Willis, had been working on it for almost three years. He had regarded it almost as a hobby, to be indulged in while his normal activities (which included the making of new films) went on as usual. There was a justification for this approach: manipulating old footage and working on special effects required a lot of time, sometimes months for just a few seconds of film. Now he enjoyed the fruits of his labours. 'I had come to bury Woody Allen once and for all, and I had stayed to praise him,' wrote Andrew Sarris in the *Village Voice*. 'A welcome wooing of sensibility and intellect,' was how Richard Schickel defined it in *Time*. And the *Newsweek* critic, Jack Kroll, recognised Woody as 'Our most intelligent comic and most comic intelligence.'

Broadway Danny Rose and *The Purple Rose of Cairo* followed. Both films were successful and greeted by some with praise and panegyrics, and by others with criticism and condemnation. There was even someone who linked the titles of the two films and joked: 'This is Woody Allen's rosy period.'

Which just goes to show that years of pouring out puns puts you at risk that someone will repay you in kind sooner or later!

Another moment of great consonance between the film-maker and his public came with the release of *Hannah And Her Sisters*, a kind of *Manhattan* in colour, full of grace and spirit. Interminable queues of people formed outside cinemas to see *Hannah*, and both the New York Film Critics Circle and the Los Angeles Film Critics Association declared it to be The Best Film of 1986. And while *Radio Days*, the film of 1987, was already successfully pulling in the cinema audiences, *Hannah* was presented at the Academy awards ceremony in Hollywood laden with nominations and subsequently won three Oscars for the most original screenplay, best supporting actress (Diane Wiest) and best supporting actor (Michael Caine).

Anti-Hero
WOODY ALLEN

Woody as a gangster, Woody among guer-illas, Woody and the ghost of Bogart. Woody and sex, Woody in the future, Woody against Napoleon Bonaparte. This is the first chapter in his film-making career, and the one in which he presents himself as a 'classic' comedian: so classic, in fact, as to appear always as a fixed character, as the tradition requires. 'Woody,' the neurotic, bungling, little man, is from the same family as the sentimental tramp (Chaplin), as the man who never smiles (Keaton), and the bespectacled optimist (Lloyd). Even the style is less that of comedy than of farce, in that slapstick vein which runs from 1910 (Mack Sennett) on through to Jerry Lewis. Moreover, one even gets the impression that Woody Allen is striving consciously to bring back the old forms and methods for making people laugh, amalgamated, obviously, with his own original creative ideas and adapted to the times. In such a thoughtful creator as Allen, we should not find this at all surprising.

Who then, precisely, is this bungling, neurotic little man? The alter ego of the director, of course; but above all he is a 'schlemiel.'

'The schlemiel,' according to a Jewish proverb, 'falls on his back and breaks his nose.' He is perhaps the most popular of all the 'masks' that Yiddish folklore has created and perpetuated in the theatre and the literature of the Jews of the Kiaspora: he is incurably clumsy, his nature is to blunder, and he stumbles, against his will, but unerringly, into every problematic situation conceivable. The character of Woody Allen was formed from these elements, and so, to a greater or lesser degree, were those of other Jewish artists like Danny Kaye or Jerry Lewis. As defined by the scholar Jean-Pierre Coursodon, the schlemiel corresponded to the character of a typical hero of the comic cinema. 'An incompetent who

saved himself from being bullied to extinction through his own endless cunning and, paradoxi-cally, enormous creative impulse.' He is the victim of readily identifiable enemies, such as the myth of success, sexual urges, inanimate objects, mass communication – they 'beat' Woody every time; and every time he gets up cheerfully and tries again.

The truth is that he has a deep-seated need for success, for women, for things. If they are denied to him, he has no choice but to renew his efforts to gain them; he must satisfy his neurosis or perish. This is what distinguishes Allen's heroes from the heroes of the comic cinema of the Twenties or Thirties. They were eccentric, unusual, but perfectly content to be themselves. They opposed, on equal terms, a world which was different to them, and from this clash burst forth laughter.

'Woody,' too, is a deviant character, but he is also vulnerable: he is a victim of this world that is different from himself, though in a certain sense he is integrated, a by-product of this wealthy, modern society.

Another new element is the hero's level of intel-lect. Even though he is invariably presented as a clumsy fool, Allen's hero always ends up playing the role of an intellectual or a leader, thrust into a situation in which the people who surround him are even more unprepared than he is. In the wake of so many men of action in so many adventure films, this is the thinking man taking his revenge, even if the setting is purely burlesque. In a mock heroic sense, his experiences illustrate the coming of age of the 'eggheads' in American society.

'I don't dwell on love too much because it can be sentimental. Chaplin sometimes was too senti-mental. The audience comes to see me and laugh,' wrote Woody Allen in 1975. He denied, however, that his characters disdained sentiment and pointed out that the hero was in love in *Play It Again, Sam*, in *Take The Money And Run*, and in *Bananas* and *Sleeper*. With his nineteenth century sensibilities Chaplin put love on a pedestal and would never have dreamt of making it a subject for laughter. Allen laughs at it: with his dialogues between lovers

Woody Allen with Herb Hall. From the very beginning
of the Seventies, the actor-director has regularly
performed, every Monday evening, as a clarinettist at
Michael's Pub in New York.

who no longer understand each other (*Bananas*),
with the embarrasement of the husband who cannot
undo his wife's dressing-gown (*Take The Money
And Run*), at the little awkwardnesses of physical
love, like the cramps (*Take The Money . . .*), or the
need to think of an athlete in action to feel more
potent (*Play It Again, Sam*). Even in his relationships with women, the neurotic schlemiel fulfills his
destiny as a bungler. It is worth bearing in mind,
however, that the irony is directed exclusively at
the character's behaviour and not at the feelings
themselves. In fact, human relationships are treated
as very precious in the artistic world of Woody
Allen. To a great extent his later works revolve
around this central idea. Like his predecessors,
Allen's heroes are solitary figures or, even worse,
isolated. For them, the quest for a woman is endless:
the only possible escape from alienation and neurosis. It is significant that this quest is accompanied
from time to time by 'chivalrous' attitudes. For
instance, there is Virgil's attempt to return to the
straight and narrow in *Take The Money And Run*;
there is Fielding's deep longing for success to please
a beautiful woman in *Bananas*, Allen's personal
sacrifice in the best interests of the girl in *Play It
Again, Sam*, Miles' completion of a dangerous
mission in *Sleeper*, and the same in *Love And
Death*. Small and isolated, this hero has no friends
of his own sex, or else he never manages to feel at
ease with them; he only reaches a state of equilibrium, at last, when he finds a mate.

The Allen Woman, for her part, is not a motherly
figure offering protection to men in distress, as one
might have been led to believe. On the contrary, she
has the same weaknesses and idiosyncrasies as her
male counterpart: in general, she is insecure, sometimes she stammers (*Take The Money And Run*), or
lives on tranquilisers (*Play It Again, Sam*), or has fits
of hysteria (*Sleeper*), or she finds consolation in
nymphomania (*Love And Death*). The man–woman
relationship is, because of their shared weakness,
one of perfect equality. Springing from a technological, depressed era in society, theirs is a bond to
help two people overcome common adversity, to

better sustain them in the coldness of social
relations.

The relationships with women demonstrate the
one human emotion which the director openly
endorses, and which he excludes from the scepticism
which permeates all his work: kindness. This, too,
will be much more marked in the later films, but it is
worth noting at least two significant moments in
this initial phase of his early work: the walk on the
beach in *Play It Again, Sam* (the main character has
brought a small present for Linda, a little plastic
animal), and the conversation after lunch in *Sleeper*
(where Miles talks about himself, about joking as a
defence mechanism, and the need for a degree of
affectionate warmth to give life to a sexual relationship). These are gracefully elegant passages, in
which the character manifests his real nature: his
genuine gentleness and his fundamental inability to
think badly of anyone or do them harm. We are a
long way in this from the corrosive Marx Brothers
and the often teasing Chaplin. Instead, we get a
glimpse in the background of the figure of Buster
Keaton.

Woody Allen is 'camp'. This expression was
coined by the New York intellectuals in the Fifties,
the same New York that produced the most famous
comedians, the most caustic playwrights, cartoon-
ists like Jules Feiffer, and the alternative 'under-
ground' movement. Briefly, 'camp' is a type of
aestheticism which finds pleasure in works that are
either vulgar, or 'arty', as viewed from a high level
of aesthetic appreciation. It is not so much the
work itself which is enjoyed, rather one's own
condescending appreciation of it; rather than
admire the author, it is his clumsy attempt to be
an author which is savoured. Thus the university
professors who collect Flash Gordon comics and
plastic souvenirs are motivated by a 'camp'
sensitivity.

This attitude was born of the meeting between
the intellectual aristocracy of New England and the
rising tide of mass culture: comics, films, television.
Instead of taking refuge in studies for select minority
groups, these intellectual patricians gave their

support to the new 'artistic'-phenomena: although it was not possible, of course, for them to appreciate them in the same unsophisticated way as the mass audience to which they were directed. A new kind of snobbery came about as a result of this. The films of Woody Allen, in fact, all his creative output up to the middle of the Seventies, have close, obvious relationships with 'camp.' Typical, for example, is the wide and seemingly unconnected spread of cultural references, which in Allen's work ranges from Hassidic legends to the sports pages, from Kierkegaard to Mickey Spillane, from Eisenstein to Michael Curtiz. Also typical of 'camp' are both the very obvious scepticism in his work and his refusal to take up any precise political standpoint. But, of course, though the 'camp' element is one aspect of Allen's work, even in the early stages of his career, his work as a whole could never be defined as 'campy', for the reason mentioned at the outset, something which was truly 'camp', attempted, but failed completely to achieve a high cultural level. Woody Allen's work could not possibly be categorised in this way and his films in particular are completely 'auteur' films.

They can be more easily spoken of as Pop Art Cinema. Artists such as Rauschenberg, Lichtenstein and Johns were not without certain 'camp' qualities and while Allen was proving himself as a comedian they were 'quoting' in their paintings pieces of 'popular' work, work designed for mass consumption. The elite were appropriating popular culture to themselves. The mass market element in Batman or a hamburger was given enhanced value by presenting Batman or the hamburger with the same aesthetic effort and attention which was given, in other ages, to paintings of horsemen with their hounds or Victorian worthies.

Naturally, all this had its ironic aspect: taking the consumer-orientated object out of its context and putting it in a more intellectual setting only highlighted in a ruthless way the intrinsic shallowness of the object in the first place.

Allen's early films, full of scenes and quotes from other films (frequently of the 'popular' kind), have much of this in them. Pop art spread the use of collage as a technical method; and collage ('the form of art which is basic to our time,' according to the writer Donald Barthelme) is the technique fundamental to the 'formless comedy' exemplified and practised by Woody Allen. Pop paintings and the films of Allen are further related in that both choose to describe not so much natural reality as human creations: the paintings are derived from comics, design, illustrated magazines; the films are derived from other films, television, advertising. In the two cases, the intentions were different: pop artists carried out their stylistic exercises on single themes, such as mass market consumption, or industrial products, and there their interest ended. Allen, on the other hand, composed his works 'by means of' the products of modern mass civilisation, and he employed them for different purposes, above all as a vehicle for his own personal inventions.

For about fifteen years it was almost obligatory for any decent Western film-maker to insert allusions and references to other films and directors in their films. It was partly a game played amongst friends and partly a way of expressing oneself. This fashion was born in the 'Nouvelle Vague' cinema in France, where there were many fanatical ex-film-goers working, all in love with the history and the world of the cinema. It then spread quickly through the new European and American cinema.

These references could range from a direct quote from a work or a straight imitation of a famous scene, to simply naming a director or a film in the dialogue. They could range from parody to actually making a film 'in the style of' some earlier master. Truffaut, Godard, Malle, Varda, Bertolucci, Bogdanovich, Scorsese and De Palma were all, at different times, exponents of this technique.

The key to Woody Allen's quotations (his films are, at times, patchworks of pieces borrowed from other films) is probably supplied by *Play It Again, Sam*. In this work, cinema and reality identify with each other. For Allan Felix, film critic and cinema lover, Humphrey Bogart is a tangible presence and not an image on the screen. He tries to imitate

Bogart's behaviour and he envies him his success. When he dreams, Allan Felix does not dream of things as they could be, but rather as they would be in a film. His wife runs off with a hippy on a motor bike and both of them look as though they came from *Easy Rider*. Dick goes to drown himself in the ocean as if he were playing in *A Star Is Born*. It is significant that Allen has chosen Humphrey Bogart, the idol of his own generation, as the ideal model for his character. This is a give-away sign of the great similarity in tastes and choices (and this view is supported by the evidence of many friends and colleagues) between the creator, Woody Allen, and his creation Allan Felix. Both of them interpret reality in terms of the cinema, and the cinema in terms of reality. Regardless of the name he is given for his different appearances on the screen, the character depicted by Allen in his earlier works, is always the offspring of, and the standard bearer for, the fusion between everyday reality and the collective imagination. As a consequence, it is only logical that his stories are told by means of quotations from films or television shows.

This meant that Woody Allen as a film director did not have to be very rigorous in his choices. And it mattered little, in this case, if the quotation was deliberate (like the perambulator that bounces down the stairs in *Bananas* which is a clear reference to *Battleship Potemkin*), or so vague as to be perhaps unintentional (like a passage in *Play It Again, Sam*, where the girl threatens Bogart with a revolver, which owes something to *The Maltese Falcon*).

This also explains Allen's type of quotation, which is almost never literal. In fact, the only instance of literal quotation is the insertion in *Play It Again, Sam* of the finale from *Casablanca*. All other 'quotation' in Allen's work is in the form of remake, or parody, or allusion, like the Antonioni-type episode in *Everything You Always Wanted To Know About Sex . . .*, or the Bergman-type dreams in *Bananas* and *Love And Death*, or the Chaplinesque scenes in the same two films.

The impression given is that this whole network of cross-references does not have any scholarly significance: that it is not the result of deliberate idealogical or cultural choices from cinematographic history. It seems, rather, to be of simple biographical origin, as, for example, with the choice of Bogart (somebody ten years older might have thought of Gary Cooper, somebody ten years younger might have thought of James Dean). In effect, it is all a 'private joke' of huge dimensions: it is a wink, a nod of understanding, to his contemporaries, and to those who shared his experiences as a cinemagoer, which has been opened out to an entire public. In this his first creative phase, Woody Allen was very definitely both representing and carrying the flag for the New York male of his generation, sub species 'comic'. Richard Schickel, one of the best critics of American cinema, wrote: 'Listening to his public monologues has always given me and mine the peculiar sensation that our own interior monologues have been tapped and are being broadcast . . . "Woody Allen c'est moi", any of us could say. For, indeed, we had been shaped by all that had shaped him. . . . We were the first generation to accept the psychoanalytic metaphor easily, naturally and, above all, youthfully. A lot of us, like Allen, acquired our first shrinks at the time we acquired our first jobs. And, one suspects, for much the same reason, which is that reality failed to match expectations. . . . Beyond their obvious gifts, the most appealing quality of the comedians of the Nineteen Sixties was the fact that their public personas bore some relationship to their private selves. . . . Nor were there teams of anonymous gag writers mediating the exchange between performer and audience. And this suited us very well, for we may have been the last generation of educated Americans with a strong faith in the value of the singular voice speaking singly. . . . *Our* tradition: some 30 years of slumping farther and farther down on our spines while the great screen before us flickered with uncounted tales of crime and espionage. College may have made us appreciators of literary modernism, but the matinées of childhood maddened us with movies – and were the first

Woody at the piano. Allen's comedy tends towards nonsense, but at the same time he has shown himself well able to use and update the classic repertoire of comic devices developed by the comedians of the early decades of this century.

on the scene. . . . His (Woody Allen's) work . . . has been shot full of ever more brilliant comment on the heritage that is, shall we say, the mother and father of us all.'

No discussion of Woody Allen's work would be complete without reference to his use of parody. It serves a double function. On the one hand it is used, as it normally is, to play a game with the material to which it relates: to take one out of many examples, consider a story like *A Twenties Memory*, in which Hemingway's literary material and style are taken to ridiculous lengths. In its second form of usage, parody serves as a support.

The humour which is characteristic of Allen is abstract, heading towards 'nonsense': something rational is therefore essential to it. A good example, remaining with Allen's literary work, would be a tale like *The Schmeed Memoirs*, in which Hitler's barber recounts the story of Nazism and the Second World War as if it were merely a question of shampoo and sideburns. In precisely the same way, Allen's early cinema is inspired in dazzling moments of brief duration, but it lacks substance and visibly fails to deliver the goods every time it comes to narrating a plausible story. At such moments it is the parody which saves it. Whoever has the time and patience will notice, upon study, that on innumerable occasions in these early works the subject of the film or even sequences in it are not 'original,' but are actually based on some previous work.

All of this allows Allen a further advantage: he can use clichés with impunity, since clichés themselves must be the raw material for a parody of them. And lastly, he can allow himself the luxury of composing his film in an elliptical manner, without having to develop the details: the audience already knows the story line.

The comedians of the Golden Age of Comedy (the three decades from 1910 to 1940) possessed, over and above what they invented spontaneously, a large repertoire of standard devices for provoking laughter. Each of these devices had its own name; and if some of them were completely individual, like the tie twiddle of Oliver Hardy, many others made

up a common patrimony. They formed a kind of 'intellectual code of laughter,' which needed only to be expressed to give a form to the comic discourse. From his very first attempts, Woody Allen, reopened the great treasure chest of this cinema and this culture.

The 'take' is the comical reaction of someone who finds himself in an unexpected situation. Virgil Starkwell, in *Take The Money And Run*, talks about a robbery to a man he believes to be a fellow criminal, but then realises that he is a policeman. 'Double take': faced with an unexpected situation, the character's first reaction is to behave as if everything were normal and only after a few moments does he 'understand.' In *Sleeper*, Miles Monroe laughs at the news that he has been awakened after two hundred years, and then he falls into a dead faint when he realises that it is the truth. The 'camera-look' is the breaking of cinematographic convention, when the character addresses himself directly to the spectator. In *Everything You Always Wanted To Know About Sex . . .*, Woody, the court jester, turns to the public after eluding two guards and says, 'Did you see how I made a fool of them?' 'Deadpan' consists of showing no reaction in circumstances which would normally cause agitation or excitement. In *Take The Money . . .*, Virgil asks a massive black man, who has been similarly condemned to forced labour, to strike off his chains with the sledgehammer; and Virgil remains impassive when the Negro misses the chain and strikes him on the foot. The 'pratfall' is a spectacular fall; and in *Sleeper*, Miles slips over and over again on a giant banana skin.

There are also innumerable 'surprise' gags, as, in *Bananas*, with the throwing of the hand grenade: Fielding Mellish is confused, he throws the pin instead and the grenade explodes in his hand; immediately afterwards he tries again, having learnt his lesson; he throws the grenade and the pin explodes in his hand! The battle with inanimate objects is another constant theme. Comedians of the past were victims of doors which slammed perversely in their faces, of automobiles which fell apart, and of mechanical instruments which behaved in every way except that for which they were designed; and Woody has frequent problems with wardrobes which empty themselves on top of him, with rifles which refuse to be assembled, with cars that he cannot drive, and so on.

In this field, one can say that Woody Allen is at the least eclectic in his choice of themes. Any coherence in the nature of his comedy springs more from his own physical appearance and personality as an actor than from a precise and well-defined range of procedures.

There is a kind of trademark, and it consists of the 'throwaway' or the 'one-liner.' The former consists of showing, in the background of a scene, action which is different and completely incongrous to the action being shown in the foreground. There are examples in *Take The Money And Run*, *Bananas*, and *Love And Death*. The most brilliant example of all, perhaps, is in the old *What's New, Pussycat?*: a character similar to Toulouse-Lautrec sits down in a bar: Allen and O'Toole arrive and while they dominate the scene, Lautrec sits quietly at his little table with . . . Emile Zola, Paul Gauguin and Vincent Van Gogh! The 'one-liner' is a surprise joke, in few words, thrown in nonchalantly when the audience least expect it. This acts, of course, as a verbal technique rather than a visual one, and it is used in great profusion. From the very beginning, it has been the principal comic element in Allen's work. 'I'm mulatto: my father is negro, my mother is white and vice versa'. 'The CIA doesn't run risks: half of its men fight for the revolution, the other half fight against it.' 'I can sneeze backwards and balance on an eye.' There are innumerable other examples, because the 'one-liner' permeates almost every one of his films from both his earlier and later work.

Finally, one other distinctive element is worth noting in Allen's work and that is the insistent and almost systematic use of the 'private joke,' an allusion which means nothing except to a few initiates. This is not new, of course: generations of writers and actors have filled their works with private winks and nudges to their friends. Amongst the comedians were Laurel and Hardy, and Jerry Lewis, to name a few. In Allen, however, this tendency is taken so far as to become almost affectation. In *Sleeper*, at a certain point, it is reported that the Third World War broke out when Albert Shanker gained control of the atomic bomb; and outside of the New York audience nobody had heard of Albert Shanker, a picturesque and combatative character, who was head of the local teachers' union. In the same film, the psychodrama during which Miles Monroe relives a lunch at his parents' house is full of authentic details, such as his address in Flatbush and his pending divorce. In *Zelig* the female protagonist is called Eudora Fletcher, after the headmistress of the secondary school which Allen attended in the Forties. We could go on and on listing examples.

Probably Woody Allen's most original and durable contribution to comedy, in cinema and literature, is the achievement of certain abstract moments which are striking in the clarity of their absurdity. Many examples have already been instanced, but there are others such as the prisoner condemned to be locked up with a life insurance salesman, or of the whipping given not to the prisoner but to his shadow (*Take The Money*), also certain short stories like *The Discovery And The Use of The Fake Ink Blot*. These rarefied inventions do not have the same impact on the audience as that created by more coarse and explicit devices. We tend to laugh more at Woody trying to help someone to park a car properly (and causing it to crash in the process), than seeing him transformed into a rabbi through the effects of the medicine he is taking. But these original ideas are inventions which hold the charm of the 'jamais vu,' and fascinate us by showing us glimpses of a pure, creative imagination at work.

The second period in Allen's work began in 1977 with *Annie Hall*. The transition did not take place suddenly. On the contrary, it is easy to see the signs of a slow maturing of themes and style in several of the preceding films. But the transformation, from here onwards, is quite clear: from farcical, 'slapstick' comedy to the 'comedy of manners' (a comedy of morality, or to be more exact, here, a comedy of behaviour). Alvy Singer, protagonist of *Annie Hall*, is not related to Virgil Starkwell or Fielding Mellish or Miles Monroe. They are 'masks', puppets in a fairy tale, invented at a typewriter. As is perfectly proper and correct in that kind of art form, they are caricatured characters in caricatured situations. Alvy Singer, and after him, Ike Davis (*Manhattan*) or Sandy Bates (*Stardust Memories*) are complete, rounded characters involved in situations and events which are not full of great drama, but are endowed instead with the shades and contradictions of real life.

From 1977 onwards, Woody Allen's alter ego on the screen would mirror the evolution which pushed him in film after film to change the style and the basic themes. Each new work was apparently only vaguely related to the others; but in each one there is the unifying element of the author's own personality, never tired of portraying itself in the diverse moments of its existence and in all its varied facets. The sum of all these countenances makes up a kind of self-portrait, in the style of Francis Bacon: a self portrait of a particular man, at a particular time, in a particular society.

There is, to further mark the transition, a very noticeable psychological change: the reaching of maturity. The Woody Allen character is no longer a solitary young man, who is looking for a soul-mate: he is an adult who shares intense and difficult relationships with his partners. He no longer models his behaviour on the cultural stereotypes offered by others (the gangster, the political militant, the intellectual). On the contrary, he now strongly puts his own views to the forefront (we think at once of Ike Davis' reasons for living in *Manhattan*, or of the long odyssey of Leonard Zelig in the film of that name). Formerly, in his cabaret performances and in his films as a director, the comic personality that was Allen laughed at himself and put himself in front of the audience in order to shield his real nature from their judgement. In the films, he protected himself when dealing with major themes like love, death and fellowship by means of humourous situations. *Annie Hall*, in complete contrast, is

not only self-revealing but also self-wounding in the way it frankly depicts certain facts from Woody Allen's real life.

In *Manhattan*, the personality of Ike Davis is so vulnerable as to appear ridiculous on a number of occasions: and yet he is presented on film to the audience, with vulnerability, with candour, with involvement. This does not mean that laughter has been banished in this second period. It has simply ceased to be the distorting lens through which we see reality. Above all, it has ceased to be the smoked glass behind which the author hides his true face.

On stage, *Play It Again, Sam* was a lot less playful than the film which was taken from it. Its narrative structure was much more solid than in the film which Allen made in the same period, and it was not without its ethical points nor a certain lyricism of its own. It is easy to see that, barring a few details, the Ike Davis of *Manhattan* is the Allan Felix of the stage, grown ten years older (which is the time lapse between one work and the other). And then *Death*, a one act play written in 1975, on the subject of the urban malaise and the search for identity, although sprinkled with witty comments, was a fundamentally serious work.

The spiritual equilibrium achieved by Woody Allen has permitted him to transfer this style and inspiration from the more restricted environment of the theatre to the much wider but more difficult environment of the cinema (curiously enough, his work as a comic writer was never subjected to any repudiation and he continued to produce works openly comic in intent).

In this new period, Woody Allen has given up studying his navel, and turns his attention to other beings, their habits and their lifestyles. Henceforth, sometimes treated lightly, sometimes seriously (*Interiors*) he depicts humanity in microcosm, a place, a town (*Manhattan*) or even an epoch (*Zelig*).

Having come out of his shell, Allen shows an ethical conscience in addition to his artistic conscience. Even at the risk of appearing to sermonise, from this point on he bears witness to his times and even proposes his own diagnosis for them.

Charlie Chaplin's name comes to mind right away. His career path and his choices present a number of analogies with those of Woody Allen. Each directed a powerful dramatic film without acting in it (*Interiors*, Allen; and *A Woman of Paris*, Chaplin); *Manhattan* is like *City Lights*, a tale of urban anxiety made sweet in the end by a woman's smile; *Stardust Memories* is a momentary outburst of harsh and ungenerous humour like *Monsieur Verdaux*; and why not hazard a suggestion that his strange love story, his evocation of a whole epoch, his parable of sickness to health, *Zelig*, is like a combination of *Modern Times* and *Limelight*.

There is no doubt that at a certain point in his career Allen was struck by what has been called 'the Chaplin Syndrome:' the clown's need to wash the make-up from his face and become a dramatic writer and a prophet. In these years of transition in particular, interviews with Allen are filled with references to Chaplin, in sharp contrast to Allen's earlier eulogies to comedy as an end in itself.

Chaplin, however, served only as a point of reference for the content. From the point of view of style, there had to be other influences. These were primarily Bergman and Fellini whom he idolised, and, with hindsight, a number of other European film-makers. Woody Allen's new cinema ended up being almost completely outside the American tradition, and becoming an original mixture of European (mainly North European) and New York sensibility.

Bergman's influence was notable. It was said that *Annie Hall* was *Scenes From Married Life* set in New York, and that *A Midsummer Night's Sex Comedy* was a remake of *Smiles On A Summer's Night*; and it was also said that *Interiors* was the only Bergman film that had not been directed by Bergman!

Certainly, Fellini was influential. *Stardust Memories* is so like Fellini in style that one could almost call it a prose version of *8 1/2*. But Allen's reference to these masters is much more mature and fertile than in his earlier films. Here, we are no longer talking about homage or parody, but rather an eclectic ability to absorb and reproduce certain ways of shooting scenes according to the specific themes being dealt with.

How better to describe, other than in the style of Bergman, the obsessive agoraphobia of a wealthy urban family plagued with internal tensions. Allen's ability to assimilate other influences constitutes a style in its own right; but in addition there now exists an Allen style that owes nothing to anybody (*Manhattan*), stemming from an intellect perfectly capable of making choices and decisions with extraordinary rigour and versatility, from the use of seemingly 'out of date' techniques like black and white filming to the cinematic illusionism of *Zelig*.

'For every ten Jews who suffer and complain,' says one proverb, 'God creates an eleventh to make them laugh.' Throughout the whole world in the performing arts and literature of the last two centuries, we have witnessed such an outpouring of Jewish comedy and comedians that the particular sensibilities of this people have often, without us realising it, ended up by being accepted as common to us all. Is there a Jewish school to which Allen may be said to belong? Some have maintained this view, while others, the vast majority, have denied it. 'It doesn't exist as such', declared Mel Brooks, for example. 'It so happens that me, Jerry Lewis and Woody Allen are Jewish, and that's all. But Buster Keaton and Laurel and Hardy weren't Jewish'.

In truth, it seems that Allen belongs much more to the great 'American' tradition of humourists and comedians. In this tradition, the Jewish predilection for the play on words, for the 'wisecrack' (a sharp, intelligent, witty remark), and for self-irony, has come to be accepted as a fundamental component. It is worth noting that the technique of paradox so dear to Allen, and so beloved of Jewish humourists, goes back to the English tradition (Oscar Wilde was a master of this art: 'When one tells the truth, sooner or later one is certain to be found out.' 'Before certain death scenes it is necessary to have a heart of stone to avoid bursting into laughter'). The repartee which we enjoy so much in *Annie Hall* or *Manhattan* reminds us of the sparkling scenes which

enlivened so many 'light' American films, scenes which so often owed their success to the skills of Jewish comedy script writers.

This ethnic identity surfaces from time to time in the work of the film-maker from Flatbush. His obsession with the Holocaust will not leave him. The Nazis and, above all, the demoniacal figure of Hitler are constantly in the foreground, from the cabaret monologues of the early Sixties up to the scenes in *Zelig* set in Germany. In many little details, the character played by Allen on the screen is almost always recognisable as a Jew. *Annie Hall* is an explicit expression of the contrast between that part of America which is poor, frustrated and Jewish (Alvy's family) and the much larger part of rich, impassive, Gentile America (Annie's family). But in the course of the years these references have become steadily more rare and Allen has always denied this theme with a consistent exasperation in his conversations with journalists. In fact, throughout his career, he has always had about him very little of the 'ethnic' showman, the entertainer who interprets and laughs at the faults and clichés of his own race and who speaks, in the main, to those of his own religion and background. Despite being brought up in a devout and traditional family, Allen has always refrained from typically Jewish manifestations. So much so that his undenominational character has often displeased orthodox and practising Jews, and the biting references here and there in his films and books have often aroused resentment and earned him the odd epithet 'Jewish anti-Semite.'

This break with his origins has not been replaced with any new attachments. Half way between a minority culture that he has deliberately left behind and a majority culture around him (a 'WASP' culture, White Anglo-Saxon Protestant, superficial and pragmatic) that does not enchant him, Woody Allen bets everything on the individual, on the personal development of self. In this he puts himself alongside Philip Roth, Saul Bellow, Bernard Malamud, and Joseph Heller. Those writers with the same ethnic roots, the same cultural backgrounds, react to insecurity in the same way,

through individuality and a heightened sensitivity.

In this sense then, Allen does belong to a tradition, but a very recent tradition, still developing. The words of Saul Bellow (in *Herzog*) could have been written for Allen, 'This is the story of my life: how I rose from humble origins to complete disaster.' And when, in Philip Roth's book, Alexander Portnoy sighs: 'America, America . . . America for me is an Aryan girl tugging on my arm whispering my love, my love, my love, my love!' one can almost see Woody Allen with Diane Keaton. The schlemiel is the central character for all these writers. Like that of Allen, he is a masochist deprived of certainty, but full of desires, sexual desires above all. Sensitive, vulnerable, intelligent. Exposed, like a photographic plate to capture the image of his times, his own problems of existence.

And if Claudio Magri writes, behind these authors we can glimpse the shadows of their ancestors, the representatives of the great world of Yiddish or Jewish-American literature, then we can also trace the genealogy of this cosmopolitan, city dwelling, film-maker, behind whom lurk the shadows of Cholem-Aléikhem with his *Tevje The Milkman*, of the actor Lowy who enchanted Kafka with his ramshackle troupe of players, of ghettos full of wry 'masks' and anguish about the meaning of life. A culture inherited in the blood, which combines in various ways with Bergman and Fellini, with Camus and Kierkegaard, with Freud and Jung.

Despite the hilarity which it aroused in the audience, Allen's early work was gloomy and pessimistic. It is commonplace to say that great comedians are often misanthropes or worse. In effect, the plot of a comedy film, behind the style that makes sure it is funny, is an accumulation of the blows of fate. Men, history, nature seem more horrible here than in any tragedy.

Whilst, however, it was easy in the other comedy classics to distinguish optimistic and positive attitudes, even when these were unfashionable, in Allen's early films one can find only nihilism, scepticism, dissatisfaction. After innumerable jokes about

God and death, the conclusion of *Love And Death* is that God might perhaps exist, but when he sends a sign (an angel who says, 'Tomorrow you will not be shot') he is wrong, either because he is mistaken, or because he is playing games with men. As far as our own life on earth is concerned, purpose is not to be found in politics, made ridiculous (whether conservative or progressive) in both *Bananas* and *Sleeper*. In the end, for Woody Allen everything that is in the public realm is miserable – but then so is everything private. As soon as he had found a mate, the characters played by Chaplin were happy and forgot all their misery, while Jerry Lewis put a damper on his incurable eccentricity. Allen's schlemiel, in contrast, in every one of his early films, at the end of the day is just as unhappy as he was before. Allen then continued to put on this tormented face, tortured as he was with doubt, even doubting his doubts: 'I do not believe in an afterlife: although I am bringing a change of underwear.' Such scepticism implies a mockery of everything and anything: of scales of values, of ethics, metaphysics, history, literature and the cinema. In a world where the only certainties are 'sex and death,' reality is illusory, and it is not surprising that it is confused with its representations on the cinema or television screens.

As the years passed, the doubt remained; what has changed are the conclusions that Woody draws from it. 'Life is a concentration camp. You're put there and there's no way out. The concentration camp is the real test. There are some who betray their best friends, and there are others who behave with incredible courage.' It is both a conscientious stand and an acceptance. Hic et nunc, one cannot escape from the camp, because we cannot escape death, what really counts is our behaviour to those around us. 'You only live once; but once is enough if you play it right,' says one character in *Interiors*. 'We have no other choice but to forgive each other,' whispers one of the sisters at the end of the same film. 'The sound of that music, and the breeze, and how beautiful Dorrie looked to me. And for one brief moment everything just seemed to come together perfectly and I felt happy. Almost indestructible, in a way,' reminisces Sandy in *Stardust Memories*. Like his beloved Bergman before him, Allen too now follows the path from God to man. He studies the alchemy of love, of friendship, of popularity, of hostility and compassion. These moments of gentleness, dispersed in the earlier films, now reach the status of poetry. He is a past-master in the art of exploring and describing human relationships with tenderness. Life continues to seem void of meaning for him, and still merits some irony. The urge to keep death at a distance remains for him 'the one thing that governs our existence.' But in the finale of *Manhattan*, we see Ike running anxiously towards the home of his fresh young love, and at the end of *Zelig*, we read that Leonard and Eudora live long and happily together.

From now on, Woody Allen elevates creative activity to the level of a positive value. That doyen of world psychoanalysts, Cesare Musatti, has remarked that Woody Allen's artistic activity has very probably had the effect of alleviating the neurosis which endless Freudian therapy had not cured. It has therefore had a decisive influence on his personal development. Whether or not this has been his experience, as a film director Woody Allen has shown steadily increasing respect in his films for the figures of artists and writers, and become increasingly sarcastic and savage towards bogus intellectuals. He has given to the creative person the role of being morally responsible vis-a-vis society. It is the combination of Leonard Zelig, when he passionately addresses his students with the words 'Be yourselves,' and Ike Davis, when he is enumerating the 'good reasons for living' (Groucho Marx, Mozart, Flaubert, Marlon Brando, Louis Armstrong . . .) that, together, present the likeness of the new Woody Allen.

The Films of
WOODY ALLEN

Take The Money And Run

As a child, Virgil Starkwell wanted to steal chewing gum like all the other tough kids on the street: but he was the only one to get caught. Later on in years, he gets involved in a gunfight with the police, only to discover that his gun is just a pistol-shaped cigarette lighter. He goes to prison for the first time. He makes an attempt to escape by threatening a guard with a false revolver he has made out of soap. But it starts raining and his gun turns into a handful of soap suds. He then agrees, in exchange for his freedom, to act as a guinea-pig in a highly dangerous medical experiment. He comes out of it relatively unscathed, suffering only one side effect, when he turns into a rabbi for several hours. Then love comes along. Virgil meets Louise, a sweet laundress, and after a quarter of an hour he realises that he is in love for eternity. After half an hour, he gives up completely the idea of stealing her handbag! However, he needs money to get married, and Virgil does not know any legal ways of making money. He goes into a bank and hands over a menacing note: 'I have a gun.' But he has written the message so badly that the bank clerk cannot read it, and it is passed from one employee to another, until eventually it reaches the bank manager. Virgil goes back to prison. He makes another escape bid, but this time his accomplices change their minds and forget to tell him, so he attempts a mass break out all by himself. He escapes with Louise and tries to go straight. An evil shrew of a woman finds out about him and blackmails him; he tries to kill her and ends up in trouble again. Cheered up by the birth of their son, the couple are continually on the run. One day Virgil returns to the idea of a bank job, and gathers a villainous-looking gang around him-

Two moments of action from the film. (Below, centre) The 'director' Fritz (Marcel Hillaire) sets up the fake filming which is designed to act as a cover for the bank robbery.

self. The assault is to take place in broad daylight, under the pretence of shooting a film. As always, it is a disaster. The victims prefer to be robbed by another gang, and Virgil ends up back in prison again. He makes a third escape, but still attached to the prisoners in his chain gang. For a fourth time, he is arrested, this time because Virgil starts babbling to a childhood friend, who is now an FBI agent, about how he makes a living.

The finale: interviewed in his cell, and asked about his future plans, our hero enquires if it is raining by any chance, as he carves a bar of soap with a blade into the shape of a pistol.

The film is made in the style of a television documentary, like the *March of Time* cinema newsreels of the Forties, or the *Cinema Verité* of the Sixties. There is a voice off screen which comentates on the scenes which purport to be documentary, and the transitional scenes are composed of interviews with those who, in one way or another, have known the hero.

The plot suffers from repetition (robberies, arrests, imprisonments), but it does have a certain coherence. It is a 'formless' ramble around a theme, in which entire scenes could be interchanged without in any way affecting the balance of the film. In fact, during the editing, that is exactly what happened. The film is structured like a slapstick comedy, a lively, fast moving farce. There is a simple basic plot, onto which are grafted a multitude of gags. These are often better on paper than on the screen: like Virgil's transformation into a rabbi, his imprisonment as a punishment, in a cell with an insurance policy salesman, his finding, in a bank vault, of a 'family of gypsies from Transylvania who are very valuable from an ethnological point of view'. In his debut as a film director, Woody is often content merely to transfer onto film his good ideas as a writer. The script abounds with gags: they pour out without interruption, from the off screen commentator, as well as in the dialogue between the characters. There are also some marvellous examples of purely visual comedy: Virgil goes up to a jewellery shop window, cuts through the glass which separates him from the precious stones, then he runs off with the piece of cut glass. He goes through a very elaborate process of dressing up for a romantic meeting, strides

Virgil Starkwell (Woody Allen), a delinquent who is
always in trouble with the police, has the good fortune
to run into love in the shape of Louise (Janet Margolin),
a gentle laundress.

Miss Blair, the blackmailer (Jacqueline Hyde), wants to make a deal with Virgil: his love in exchange for silence. And so, without success, he attempts to eliminate her.

confidently out of the apartment – only to realise that he has forgotten to put on his trousers. He tries to use the taps in the bathroom only to get tangled up in an epic 'struggle against inanimate objects', worthy of Stan Laurel or Jerry Lewis. Parodying certain types of scene from both the cinema and television, this film lays the foundations for a technique which will become a characteristic of Woody Allen's work: the pastiche. Archive documentary material is also used to comic effect. We see Nixon in the Fifties playing golf ('For a lot of people those were happy years', comments the speaker), and then Kaiser William inspecting his troops (this is not the real emperor, explains the speaker, but Virgil's grandfather dressed up; the crazy old man had a great influence on his grandson). As for cinematic reference, people can see as many of these as they are prepared to identify. There are undeniable references to *Cool Hand Luke* (the prison scenes), to *I Was A Fugitive From A Chain Gang* (the escape of the chained convicts), and to the Marx Brothers (Virgil's parents, ashamed of their son, will only allow themselves to be interviewed in Groucho masks). Even the character of Fritz, the director of the phoney scenes which were intended to cover up the bank robbery, would seem to be an acknowledgement to the director Fritz Lang, although Allen has denied this in writing. Another typical Allen trademark is the private joke, humour so subtle that only a few close friends can appreciate it. *Take The Money*

And Run affords at least one example of these. When Virgil's gang gets together to look at a film of the bank that Virgil has made in secret, a documentary precedes it (just as if they were in the cinema), *Trout Fishing In Quebec*. The producers' names are Rollins and Joffe, the agent and producer for Woody Allen.

In spite of all the weaknesses of inexpert directing, the variation in the pace and the tone of the film, and the ideas which are not fully worked out, *Take The Money And Run*, is, probably, together with *Love And Death*, the best of Allen's comedy films. It is also one of the richest in significance, in its depiction of the 'resistible rise' to nationwide fame of a talentless outlaw. Virgil Starkwell is not a true criminal, his ineptitude proves this. He is really an average man in the street, unable to cope with the concept forced on him by the society he lives in, that success is the only thing worth having. In the absence of any doubts about the basic premise, it is simply a question of him deciding in which field he will aim for success, and then achieving it. The path of crime has been open to him since childhood, why should he not continue along it? Moreover, no-one questions his behaviour from an ethical point of view; neither his wife, nor any of the other people who are interviewed (except his parents, but that is because they are also the victims of their own generation's myths, believing in hard work and the regular practice of religion).

And what about society? It is so obtuse and violent that it is unable to distinguish between a poor booby like Virgil and a real criminal. Hence the following paradox: branded as a public enemy, Virgil achieves the very 'success' that his talents would never

(Left) As a result of testing an experimental drug, Virgil is transformed into a rabbi. (Below) Virgil, with a fellow inmate (Lonnie Chapman), plans yet another escape: on this occasion, when it is postponed, everyone is warned except him.

have brought him. Added to this, the whole story is told in the language of the mass media, with its tone of false objectivity and its total inability to make critical judgements. This is the very media which has helped to form Virgil's distorted way of thinking. So, the story of a deceived man is told by the deceivers in a deceptive way.

Is *Take The Money And Run* social satire then? In part, yes. The rites and myths of our society do reveal their ridiculous and brutal aspects. But satire was certainly not Woody Allen's main purpose. In his works at least, he has always been suspicious of political and civil commitment. In reality, between failing in your duty and fame,

51

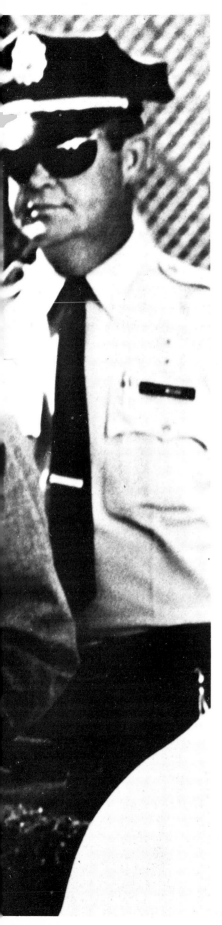

Virgil, the eternal prisoner, is comforted by the visits of
Louise. As always, he makes plans to escape.

between the blunderings of Virgil and
the dynamism of a man of action,
between the realistic investigation and
the obvious distortion of facts, there is
incongruity. And this is a particularly
powerful element in comedy. Allen
relies a lot on incongruity and he
makes us laugh a lot.

Such absurdities as these really do
exist. Each of us can prove this for
ourselves just by looking around. In
this way, the mirror that was meant to
distort turns out to be quite revealing.
It is often the case that jesters, without
even realising it, speak the truths that
no-one wants to hear.

Bananas

In the small Latin American state of San Marcos, a coup d'etat is being prepared. The event is regarded as a likeable local tradition, almost like a sporting event: to the point that it is transmitted live by American television. In the middle of the crowd, the famous American sports reporter Howard Cosell is clutching his microphone on the crowded steps of the presidential palace, awaiting the fateful moment. At last, the head of state comes out, and is punctually shot down. Cosell, forcing his way through the crowd, succeeds in obtaining an interview from him as he is expiring ('I suppose that now we will have to announce your retirement.'). The new dictator is Vargas, who outlines the new directions of his policies for the benefit of the TV audience: censorship of the press, destruction of the opposition, and so on.

Meanwhile, in New York, Fielding Mellish is at work. His job consists of acting as a guinea-pig for the strange devices invented by the company he works for. On this occasion he is struggling with the latest invention to help people keep fit during a sedentary day's work in the office. Without moving from his desk, he fills in a form, then has some basketball shooting practice, he answers the telephone and exercises his pectoral muscles; then, still sitting, he pedals an exercise cycle, until he can no longer keep up the pace and falls over flat on his back. Fielding is very unhappy and dissatisfied with his job: as he tells a colleague, he would have done better to carry on with the university: 'I had started a course on negroes. Who knows, I could have been black by now.' Instead, he is only a shy little man, and when he receives a visit that evening from Nancy, he does not know how to go about

Aspiring playboy Fielding Mellish (Woody Allen) makes
an embarrassed choice of pornographic magazines
under the disapproving gaze of a respectable customer.

courting her. Nancy is a politically
involved student who is gathering signatures against the new tyrannical
government in San Marcos. Fielding
signs at once, and then, so that he can
be near her, he takes part in picket
lines and sit-ins. But, eventually, one
day as they are walking through a
park, a setting suited to loving affirm-
ations, Nancy dumps him. Why?
Because he is immature and she has
dreams of finding a leader. Undeni-
ably, the young man leaves much to be
desired. When he tries to close a door,
he pulls the handle off; when he
makes himself a meal, he cooks the
meat with the céllophane wrapping
still on; when buying porno magazines
in a newsagents he tries to conceal
them beneath more intellectual publications (only for the salesman to
forget the prices and call out the titles
to the assistant; all in front of an old
woman who looks on in silent disapproval). Nevertheless, Fielding has
some good qualities. For example, he
is brave. When two tough guys come
into the subway carriage (one is
Sylvester Stallone, in what was almost
his debut in films), and begin to
torment an old woman, he reacts by
grabbing them by the collar and
throwing them off. He is counting on
the doors closing, and they do close,
but they also open again. A charitable
veil is drawn over the end of this
episode.

Stoically, the rejected lover does not
withdraw into himself, but instead he
decides to go on a journey to help him
to forget. Naturally, he goes to San
Marcos, the place so dear to his loved
one. As soon as he arrives, he is
invited to dinner at the palace. Not
wanting to go empty handed, he turns
up with a box of chocolates. The
president is not overjoyed (they are
milk chocolates and he prefers liqueur

flavours). But he is a generous host to his guest: he has plans to kill Fielding, put the blame on the guerillas and in this way obtain an enormous aid package from the United States. Things go badly for the president, because the guerillas kidnap Fielding and turn him into one of them. Revolution breaks out, the tyrant is overthrown and the new president is Esposito. When the villans have been brought to justice, a new era commences. Perhaps.

Esposito goes 'bananas' right away. He decides that Swedish will be the official language of the state, and that all children under the age of sixteen shall become, by law, sixteen years old. An immediate replacement is required: and who better than

Fielding. He has been to university for at least one day, so he is an intellectual giant compared to the others. And so, when Fielding, disguised behind a false beard, returns to New York in search of economic aid, he comes not just as an idiot, but with all the prestige of a head of state. Before so much glory, Nancy is completely dazzled. She tries to get close to the hero, and then ends up in bed with him . . . and when his beard turns out to be false, she complains 'I thought it was too good to be true.'

Meanwhile the law is also taking an interest in this bizarre character. His past record as a demonstrator comes to light and he is put on trial for anti-American activities. Fielding defends himself skilfully, but the witnesses

A hero in spite of himself, Fielding takes on two hoodlums in the subway. On the left is a very young Sylvester Stallone.

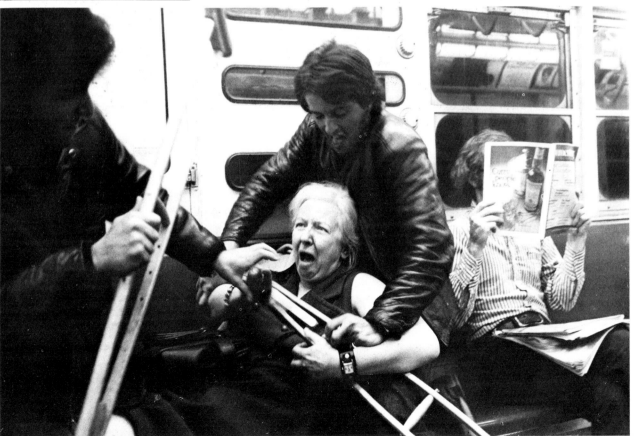

against him pile up: from the director of the FBI, J. Edgar Hoover (who, on the screen, resembles a black woman, but it seems this is just a disguise to confuse his numerous enemies), right through to Miss America, who recites like a parrot 'differences of opinion can be tolerated as long as they are not too different', and then sings Caro Nome in an indifferent soprano voice. As announced on the television evening news, after an advertisement for New Testament cigarettes (which offer a plenary indulgence), the subversive is found guilty, but the judge suspends sentence as long as Fielding promises never to go and live in his neighbourhood. So Fielding is free once again, and he returns to his beloved Nancy. He marries her. And the same Howard Cosell who had reported the San Marcos coup d'etat now commentates on the wedding night. His tone of voice and his ter-

minology are suited to a boxing match. At the end of the bout, after the ritual interviews with the contestants, Howard Cosell says farewell: 'And now they will live together happily ever after. Or maybe they won't'.

Fielding Mellish at the presidential palace in San Marcos, paying a visit to Vargas (Carlos Montalban). He brings a box of milk chocolates, but unfortunately the dictator prefers liqueur flavours.

(Below) The evil dictator Vargas makes the population pay tribute to him according to his weight. Not having any gold, diamonds or other precious objects, the poor people give what they can: horse dung.
(Right) The revolution is successful. The ministers of the fallen regime are shot in a new type of sporting competition.

The wonderful 'absurdity' of the best sequences from *Take The Money* reappears here in the best sequences of this film. At the presidential palace, dinner is served to the music of an orchestra without instruments. Fielding, delighted by the president's invitation, takes the sound of a harp to be a musical illustration of his state of mind, only to discover that it is a servant practising in a cupboard. Fielding telephones one of his collaborators who is seated in the same room as he is. When President Fielding makes his triumphant arrival at New York airport he is met by an interpreter who, instead of translating, repeats everything he says, as they are all speaking the same language. The nurses from the mental home turn up and pursue him with huge butterfly nets.

One could add to this list some brilliant courtroom scenes, and the 'mystical dream' sequence in which our hero is carried around the town, on a crucifix, and ends up having an argument with another crucified person over a parking place.

Film references are numerous. The most obvious is from *Battleship Potemkin*; from the steps of the beseiged palace an empty pram comes rolling down towards the revolutionaries (just as in the scene on the Odessa steps). There are other examples: the machine for keeping office workers fit, which leaves Fielding exhausted (the machine for eating from Chaplin's *Modern Times*); eating transformed into an erotic ceremony between Fielding and the female guerilla (Tony Richardson's *Tom Jones*); the 'mystical dream' mentioned earlier (a generic reference to Bergman); the scenes with Esposito, the crazy head of state (Rene Clair's *The Last Millionaire*). And we must not forget Woody Allen's numerous phrases and gestures which recall his beloved Groucho Marx. Of course, in *Bananas* television is also ever present, with its distorting effect on reality: the commentaries on the assassination of a politician and a night of love are both presented in totally inappropriate terms. Likewise we are shown an instance of fiction aping reality; at the moment that Cosell hands back the microphone, the camera fixes itself on his face and lingers there as he grows increasingly embarrassed.

The film has a more solid narrative framework than *Take The Money And Run*, but it is also more confused and uneven. From the point of view of

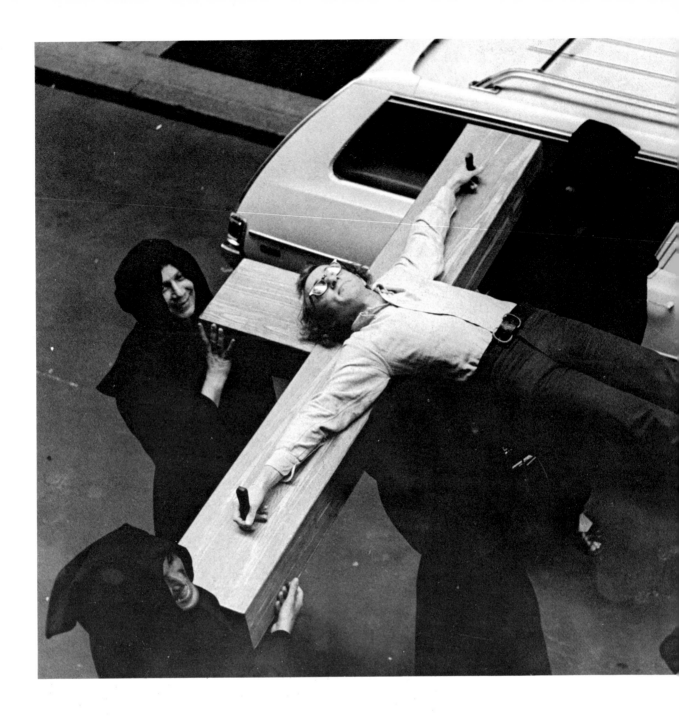

the structure, the film's main weakness lies in the loose ends that are left lying about. What happens to the victorious revolution in San Marcos? How does Fielding manage to get away from the hooligans on the subway? We never know. The scenes are cut short, and we pass on to others. Even in a 'surreal' context, the narrative ought to have a certain internal coherence. Another problem is that many of the comic inventions are gratuitous to the plot and do not help the action to flow. 'There is nothing worse than a gag out of place,' warned Buster Keaton; and in this film Woody Allen embarks on a whole series of rambling jokes and diversionary gags and, what is more, they are not always of the highest standard.

And then, if *Take The Money And Run* offered only a few elements of social satire, *Bananas* is also a long way from being a political satire. When dealing with political matters, Allen throws his punches in all directions. He makes fun of both the dictator and the guerillas, of both the CIA and the student protesters. Allen is no Swift, nor Voltaire. His funda-

Two moments of surrealistic humour.
(Left) Fielding dreams that he has trouble finding a parking place for his crucifix.
(Below) He discovers the true source of the background music.

mental view, explicitly expressed in *Sleeper*, is that politics comes down basically to a struggle for power, and the new leaders will not be any better than the old ones. All in all, the film is more derisive than satirical, because it is lacking in the basic elements of satire, that is to say moral indignation and the proposition of a different and better social order. *Bananas* pokes fun at the mania peculiar to Latin America for coup d'etats, at the ease with which the CIA gets involved ('This time the CIA's taking no chances', comment the troops that are sent to

(Below) An unwilling but confirmed batchelor, Fielding is incapable of feeding himself properly.
(Left) Nancy (Louise Lasser) gives up Fielding as a lost cause, but in the end everything is sorted out.

San Marcos. 'Half of us are with the dictator and the other half are with the rebels'), at unthinking anti-Communism, and even at political trials (Fielding is bound and gagged, just as the leader of the Black Panthers, Bobby Seale, was chained and gagged at the 'Chicago Trial' in 1969).

Finally, a word about the title of the film. *Bananas* has a triple meaning. It refers to those central American republics which are often called 'Banana Republics'; it is an echo of *Cocoanuts*, a Marx Brothers film; and in slang it has come to mean 'absurd, crazy, insane'.

Play It Again, Sam

The final scenes of Casablanca move across the screen. Humphrey Bogart, his raincoat collar turned up and a bitter gleam in his eye, make his great sacrifice for love. In' the cinema sits a small bespectacled man, with a lump in his throat in the face of such greatness of spirit. His name is Allan Felix, an unassuming film critic who spends all his time watching films and dreaming about them instead of doing anything important. But his wife has just done something very important: she has walked out on him and asked for a divorce. For what reason? Because Allan is a 'watcher', a passive character, while she is a 'doer', an active personality. Finding himself left alone in the city in the middle of August, without his psycholanalyst and without any clear idea about himself or purpose to his life, he is desperate.

Two friends, Dick and Linda Christie, come to his aid. They try to console him and find him a new companion. This is not an easy undertaking, because Allan is shy, complex-ridden and insecure. He is continually trying to emulate Humphrey Bogart, his model of virility. Bogart's vision is constantly appearing to Allan and he talks to it and turns to it for advice. Trying to create a good impression while acting as someone else is not easy, and when Allan makes the attempt with a girl friend of the Christie's, it is a total disaster: one blunder follows another and the girl makes her escape. One way or another, the female race does not seem very well disposed towards him. A notorious nymphomaniac, as soon as he lays a finger on her, pulls away, yelling, 'What do you take me for?'. A brunette he meets at the Museum of Modern Art refuses him a date because she is going to be busy com-

mitting suicide. A blonde on the dance floor hisses at him, 'Get lost, worm', and a secretary from Dick's office dumps him for some brawny motor-bikers. Only Linda, Dick's wife, can maintain with him a relationship of trust and respect. Many things draw them closer together: their sensitivity, their vulnerability, and their anxieties. Almost inevitably, an attraction grows, made easier by Dick's lifestyle, as he is completely absorbed in his work. When he goes away on business, Linda goes for dinner at the home of the involuntary bachelor. The champagne and the urging of Bogart's phantom presence overcome the couple's shyness and they spend the night together. The awakening is bitter-sweet. They really are emotionally attracted to each other, but what about Dick? Allan daydreams: Dick falls in love with an Eskimo girl and emigrates to Alaska; Dick takes it all with a stiff upper lip, like an English lord; Dick takes the news like a very jealous Italian baker; Dick gives in to despair and throws himself into the ocean. Meanwhile the real Dick has already returned home with a weight on his mind, and he loses no time in confiding in his friend. He had called home the night before and his wife wasn't there. She must be sleeping with someone else. Moreover he is not surprised, because she has been hiding something from him for some time. Now that Dick is about to fly off again on business, he has decided that he would like to take her with him to give a new start to their married life. The situation becomes clear in Allan Felix's mind. He tries to reach Linda by phone, but she is back home busy fighting with Dick. He goes to their place, but first one, then the other, have already left for the airport. He follows them. On the airport tarmac

Allan Felix (Woody Allen), the ardent admirer of Humphrey Bogart and of *Casablanca,* under a poster of the film.

They
have
a date
with
fate
in

ACADEMY
AWARD

A WARNER BROS. RE-RELEASE

PAUL   CLAUDE   SYDNEY
HENREID · RAINS · GREENSTREET · LOR

HAL B WALLIS PRODUCTION   MICH

A WARNER BROS. FIRST NATIONAL PICTURE   DIRECTED B

(Below) The vision: Allan Felix dreams of being like Bogart (Jerry Lacy), desirable to women (the actress is Mari Fletcher).
(Right) The reality: his liaison with Linda (Diane Keaton).

he catches up with the girl and he tells
her what he means to do: break off
their relationship at once. She is of the
same mind but she assures him that
she does not regret what has passed
between them. The final scene of
Casablanca is re-enacted, though in a
different form: the hero gives up his
beloved, puts his rival's mind at ease
('She came over to babysit with me
because I was lonely,' he explains to
Dick), and the plane takes off. On
the fog-shrouded runway Bogart's
phantom takes its leave. The ex-
daydreamer has matured and no
longer needs him. Of course, 'I guess',
Allan bravely explains, 'the secret's
not being you, it's being me.' And on
the screen, the credits begin to roll.

The farewell scene at the airport, a finale modelled on *Casablanca*.

The film *Casablanca* has been mentioned too many times up to now not to merit a brief résumé. As interpreted by Humphrey Bogart and Ingrid Bergman, it tells the story of Rick, an American with a mysterious but chivalrous past, and the woman he formerly loved, Ilsa. At the height of the Second World War she arrives in Casablanca with her husband Victor, hounded for his anti-Nazi activities. The feelings of the two former lovers are reawakened, but Rick draws back and protects Ilsa's husband for idealistic reasons. This 1942 success, directed by Michael Curtiz, was responsible for the revival and repopularising of an old song, *As Time Goes By*. It was Rick and Ilsa's song, sung and played in the film by Sam (Dooley Wilson), Rick's loyal, black friend. From which comes the title of Woody Allen's film *Play It Again, Sam*. The great wave of nostalgia which swept America towards the end of the Sixties and deservedly made *Casablanca* into a cult movie for devotees of the cinema rendered quite explicit Allen's rather obscure title. Of all his earlier films, *Play It Again, Sam* was by far the best received. Audiences around the world came to identify with the character of this little man, at odds with himself, disdained by women and hopelessly maladroit. This time the cinema public was not asked to watch the antics of an insubstantial character. They could really believe in Allan Felix and take his part. He became the embodiment of everyone, in any big city, who had found themselves at least once in their life not knowing who to telephone to avoid having to spend an evening alone, or who had happened to send an LP hurtling across a room by clumsily grabbing its sleeve. In this respect, *Play It Again, Sam* was a

reassuring film. It emphasises the fact that, just by being themselves, even clumsy people can show their human dignity and find a partner who understands them. The end of the film, without being too naive, was optimistic. The ordeal has been endured and tomorrow will be better. Even the most sensitive episode, Allan's seduction of Linda, did not leave any taste of bitterness. Of course it was straightforward adultery, and with his best friend's wife: but the dialogue is so acute and the acting of Woody Allen and Diane Keaton so sensitive and well thought out that one comes away with an impression of complete innocence.

It is the problem of two lonely souls which is paramount, and not the breaking of a moral contract with an absent third party.

From a formal point of view, the film is an amalgam. The basic structure is that of a sparkling comedy, with a rational plot carefully carried through, and well defined, plausible characters. Allen has taken great care with the psychology of each character, and he depicts them intelligently: Linda, tender and unsure of herself; Dick, over-involved in his work, but fundamentally human; Nancy, Allan's ex-wife who appears in his fantasies, egotistical but without spitefulness. Added to this is all the slapstick comedy of Woody Allen's early period: the overthrown furniture, the recalcitrant hair-dryer, the havoc caused in the apartment when Woody is awaiting the arrival of the girl friend introduced to him by Dick and Linda.

This is the custard pie comedy so dear at that time to Woody Allen. There is also a memorable moment of total absurdity: the hero, euphoric at having found love at last, slaps the backs of some total strangers sitting

Two attempts at seduction.
(Below) The man eater (Viva) who pulls away scandalised as soon as he touches her.
(Right) The girl he meets at the Museum of Modern Art (Diana Davila) who refuses a date with him because she has a prior engagement: she has to commit suicide.

on the parapet of a bridge. One of them is knocked right off, and without a sound, falls away into space, while Allan Felix goes imperturbably on his way.

Although this film was directed not by Woody Allen but by Herbert Ross, Allen's mark is very clear. The subject, the screenplay and the interpretation bear his signature, and the cast is made up of friends and colleagues, with whom he had played the same script in the theatre for a year and a half. Woody Allen did not have here

that 'total control' which he guarded so jealously for his own films, but his presence was so influential that reviewers have always rightly classed *Play It Again, Sam* as an Allen film. It also contains outlines of the themes and states of mind which were to become part of his style as a mature film-maker. The subtle understanding between Allan and Linda has much in common between that of Alvy and Annie in *Annie Hall*, for example. And the tender awkwardness with which Allan offers the young woman

a gift of a little plastic animal (a skunk) would not be out of character for Leonard Zelig. It is also the first film in which we could talk of a true acting performance by Woody Allen. Directed with restraint and professionalism by Ross, he does not indulge in grimaces or excessive gesticulation (as he had done, especially, in *Bananas*), and when circumstances require that he abandon the comic register, he displays moderation and subtlety. It reveals the limits of his acting ability. When he attempts to

Allen dreams of meeting his ex-wife Nancy (Susan Anspach) at the supermarket and refereeing an argument between her and Bogart. (Below) Allan the intellectual film critic, with his typewriter (and a distraction).

Another attempted seduction. In the discotheque, Allan Felix approaches a blonde (Suzanne Zenor) who contemptuously spurns him.

imitate Bogart's characteristic way of drawing back his lip up off his teeth, or narrowing the corners of his eyes, Allen's efforts are so poor as to be barely noticeable. On the other hand, he is excellent at conveying the excitement with which Allan Felix prepares for the visit of the girl that his friends are bringing to his house. His whole body is taut with emotion, his movements are brusque, he cannot keep still, he bumps into things, knocks things over.

Much of the credit for this film must also go to Diane Keaton. In *Play It Again, Sam* she interprets the first of a series of female portraits – self-portraits, which was to end in 1979 with *Manhattan*. An excellent actress, she also brings to her part a presence which is both seductive and spiritual, offering to a character as inhibited as Allan a very necessary counterweight. As for the other actors, if the performance of Tony Roberts, a veteran of Woody Allen's entourage (he was one of the actors in the stage version of *Don't Drink The Water* in 1966) is no more than creditable, Jerry Lacy's hyper-realistic imitation of Bogart is fabulous. Paramount even went as far as to buy him the costume worn by Bogart in *The Maltese Falcon*.

Everything You Always Wanted To Know About Sex, But Were Afraid To Ask

'Do aphrodisiacs work?' is the question that the first of the seven episodes in this film attempts to answer. We meet Allan Felix, the court jester in a medieval castle, who bores the king and the courtiers to distraction with his terrible jokes, and then, on the advice of his father's ghost, makes an attempt to seduce the queen. He administers a powerful aphrodisiac to her, and everything is going according to plan until he finds that the queen is wearing a chastity belt, which turns out to be totally impregnable. The king returns unexpectedly and the jester pays for his impudence with his head.

The second episode poses another question: 'What is sodomy?' It features Doug Ross (Gene Wilder), a polite, normal doctor, with a peaceful, orderly family life. One day he receives a visit from a shepherd, Stavros Milos, who has a serious emotional problem: his Armenian ewe, Daisy, does not love him anymore. He wants the doctor to talk to it and persuade it to love him again. At first perplexed, the doctor takes on the task, but, alas, the result is that he falls in love with the animal himself. His married life turns into a hell, his meetings with Daisy take place in sordid motels, and in the end he loses both the sheep he loves and his license to practise medicine. The final scene shows him in despair, sitting on the pavement like a beggar, tippling from a bottle of wool detergent.

The third episode asks, 'Why do some women have trouble reaching an orgasm?' Frabrizio and Gina are a newly wed couple from the Italian

First episode. The king (Anthony Quayle) gives the
jester, Allan Felix (Woody Allen), a good talking to.

upper class. They wear expensive
clothes, drive luxury cars, and have an
enviable standard of living. But Gina
gets no pleasure out of making love.
Fabrizio tries all possible and manage-
able solutions. At last they discover
that the wife, who is frigid in private,
becomes extremely hot blooded in
public. There follows a series of coup-
lings in rather unsuitable places, like
a restaurant, an art gallery, and an
antique shop.

The fourth episode asks, 'Are trans-
vestites homosexual?'; and it is set
among the American middle class. A
middle aged couple go with their
daughter for dinner to the house of
their future in-laws. The man (Lou
Jacobi) makes an excuse and leaves
the table, and goes up to the bedroom
of the mistress of the house, where
he puts on her clothes. He admires
himself for a long time before the
mirror, but then he hears footsteps.
Panic striken, he flees through the
window, and finds himself in the
street, where he is robbed of his handbag. Passers-by rush to his aid, the
police are called, his family and future
in-laws gather around – the situation
could not be more embarrassing. That
evening, in a maternal way, his wife
reproaches him for his vileness.

'What are sex perverts?' The fifth
episode is a parody of a typical television quiz show, compered by Jack
Barry, a genuine American television
star. In the film, the game consists of
guessing the sexual perversions of the
guests of honour, but the highpoint of
the show is the live realisation of the
most fascinating perversion of com-
petitors who have sent in letters. This

77

Sixth episode. In the clinic of Dr Bernardo (John Carradine), Victor Shakapopoulis (Woody Allen) attempts to put a halt to yet another diabolical experiment. On the left is the doctor's monstrous assistant, Igor (Ref Sanchez).

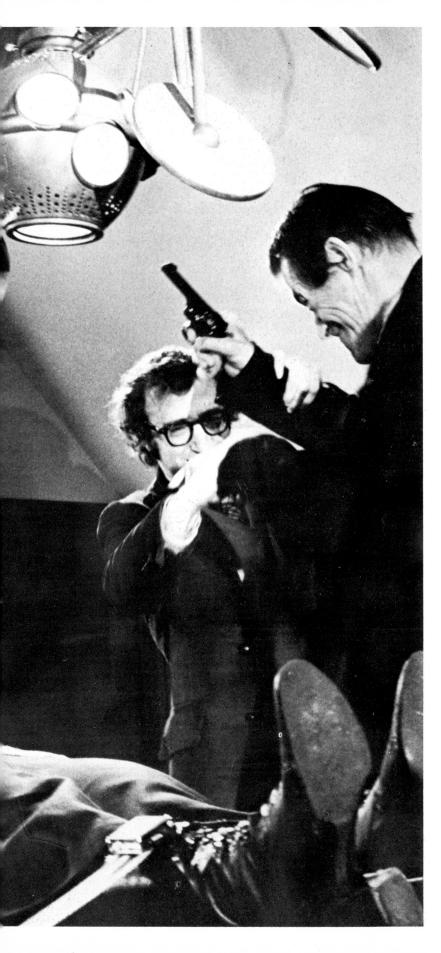

*time, the winner is an old rabbi: tied
to a chair he writhes with pleasure as
he is whipped by a beautiful blonde,
while his wife is forced to eat pork, the
forbidden meat.*

*The sixth episode is, 'Are the
findings of doctors and clinics who do
sexual research accurate?' At the
beginning, the promising young biol-
ogist Victor Shakapopoulis seems to
think so. He goes to visit a famous
sexologist, Doctor Bernardo (John
Carradine), in order to discuss with
him his research and experiments. A
blonde journalist accompanies him,
charged with interviewing the doctor.
Except that Bernardo is a scientist of
the Frankenstein genre (he even has a
misshapen assistant called Igor), and
he has plans to use his two visitors
as guinea-pigs. The result is complete
turmoil, in the course of which the
criminal genius, his dreams and even
his laboratory are annihilated. Well,
not entirely; the horror is not yet over.
Like a symbol of all the sexual
delirium which thrived in the place,
out of the ruins there arises a huge
breast. It wanders off across the
district, sowing terror and death, until
Victor cunningly manages to find a
way of capturing it by luring it into an
enormous bra.*

*The seventh and last episode is
called, 'What happens during Ejaculation?' It is set out as a science fiction
film. A futuristic control centre (the
brain) commands the operations of
the peripheral nuclei (the organs) as if
they were preparing for a space
launch. In reality, the imminent event
is sexual intercourse. To answer the
question posed by the title of the
episode, the event is seen from a male
point of view; therefore it is necessary
to make sure of an erection, eliminate
all feelings of guilt stemming from a
religious education, and enrich the*

Sixth episode. Victor in Dr Bernardo's study, with the journalist (Heather McRae) who is on an assignment to interview the celebrated researcher.

erotic stimuli. Meanwhile the sperma-tozoans are in a state of alert, ready to be launched as if they were parachut-ists. One of them (Woody Allen) is filled with metaphysical doubts and fears. In the end, the operation goes smoothly, and a celebration party is held in the control centre. Then the man is asked to do it again and they must start getting ready for a new attempt.

Fifth episode. The rabbi's (Baruch Lumet) prize-winning
perversion; he is ecstatic at being whipped by a pretty
blonde (while his wife eats pork).

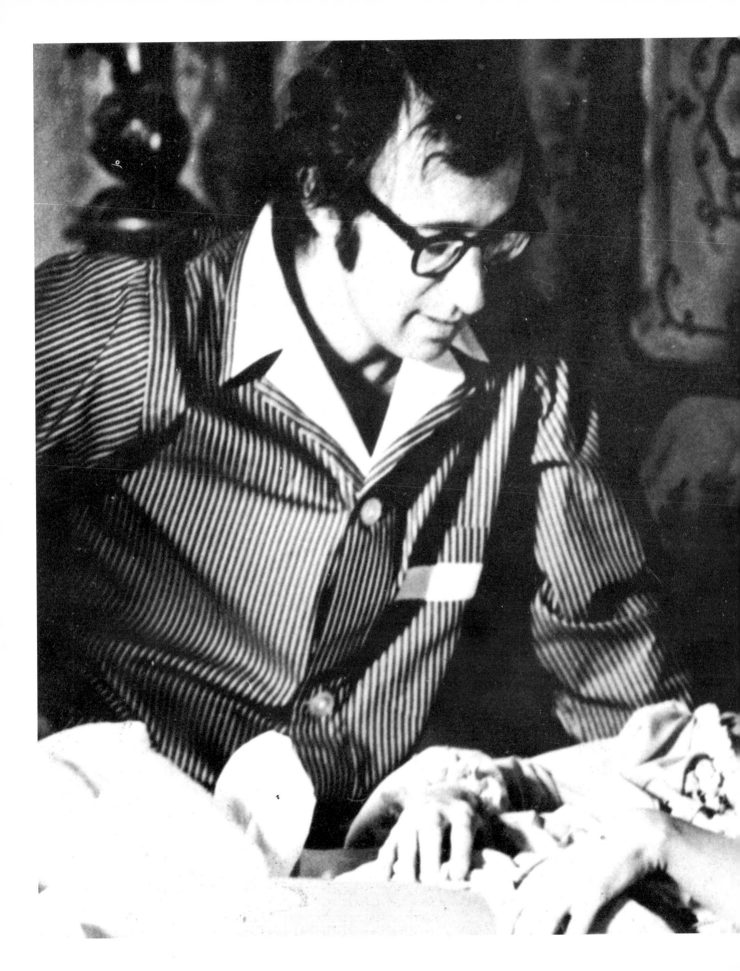

Third episode. Fabrizio (Woody Allen) and Gina (Louise Lasser) in a moment of peaceful intimacy. The young wife can only experience sexual desire in public places.

This last episode is the only really good one in the film. The pace is fast and there are plenty of good jokes ('What am I doing here?' wonders a black sperm in the midst of all the white ones). The representation of the human body as a large machine run by a high technology mission control centre, may not be original (every school book uses comparisons of this kind), but it is rich in comic consequences, like the fall of food into the stomach, or the request (to the eyes) to focus on the partner. The set designs are superb, the work of Dale Hennesy, who had previously been rewarded with an Oscar for similarly inventive human body settings in Richard Fleischer's *Fantastic Voyage*. On the whole, the subject is treated here with a refinement that is lacking in other parts of the film. Not that the film suffers from an excess of licentious scenes!: Allen is far too intelligent not to realise that the presentation of crude images would only direct the spectators' attention away from him and his setting. Nor are we dealing with a student's practical joke. Here sex has neither the healthy impetuosity of lust, nor the obsessive character of a fixation. Curiously, to tell the truth, the predominant sensation is of distance, almost of hostility. At times, the themes are dealt with in a way that is both cerebral and awkward. It seems a paradoxical thing to say but a sense of humour is often lacking. The giant breast which devours its victims with squirts of milk, the sheep which wears black stockings to please the zoophile, the rabbi ecstatic under the lash, the workers responsible for ejaculation who sing *Glory, Glory, Hallelujah* whilst floundering about up to their knees in a dubious looking liquid: these flights of the imagination create

little hilarity but a vague sense of discomfort. This is the dark side of Woody Allen's inventiveness, which was also to manifest itself again in *Stardust Memories*, a film which was also sombre and debatable.

Everything You Have Always Wanted To Know About Sex is, according to its author, a step forward on the road to true cinematic professionalism. The previous film paid little attention to 'form' (the framing, the lighting, the camera movements) and 'form' is one of the main elements of this film. The style of the episodes differs in each, because each is a parody of a different cinematic genre (in the case of the mad scientist, it is the horror film joined to second feature science fiction).

In some of the scenes, for the first time, Allen directs without appearing as an actor, and he entrusts to experienced performers like Gene Wilder and Lou Jacobi roles that he might have played himself. For the first time also, he uses not only friends, but famous names: Lynn Redgrave, Anthony Quayle, Tony Randall and Burt Reynolds. Having methodically and meticulously taught himself, Allen also begins to display versatility and sensitivity towards the image on the screen. The 'Italian' episode is a subtle imitation of Antonioni, with a bit borrowed from Bertolucci (by Allen's own admission), while the subject appears to be based more on a film by Mario Monicelli; *Casanova 1970*. In the United States, this sketch was presented with Italian dialogue and English subtitles, just like a real foreign film.

Nevertheless the directing is the real weak point of this film, which is probably the least good of all Woody Allen's output. Except for the last one, the episodes never get off the ground,

and are not very spectacular. They are often lacking in internal rhythm and, worst of all, a conclusion: they are simply cut short. The reprimand, full of connivance, to the husband who dresses up as a woman, or the dialogue between Victor and the blonde journalist in the Frankenstein episode, are makeshift, midway between sententiousness and sugary sweetness. The actors have very little space in which to move, apart from the inimitable Gene Wilder who takes advantage of his own hair-style and his tender gaze to suggest an almost sheepish image, perfect for the lover of a sheep, and an old John Carradine (unforgetable in *Stagecoach*) who offers a pleasing parody of himself in his brief appearance. Lou Jacobi is given a free rein and goes over the top. The credits at the beginning and the end of the film are very witty. They flow across pictures of rabbits – obvious allusion – mischievously accompanied by a Cole Porter song: *Let's Misbehave.*

Fourth episode. (Left) Lou Jacobi and the joys of
transvestism.
The second episode. (Below) Dr Ross (Gene Wilder)
enraptured by Daisy the sheep.

Sleeper

The year is 2173. A group of scientists accidentally discover a capsule dating back to two hundred years earlier. They open it up and inside they find a man in suspended animation, wrapped up completely, except for his glasses, in silver paper. Secretly, and with great care, he is reanimated: the ruling political regime would not look kindly on such an initiative. The man they have defrosted turns out to be Miles Monroe, an ex-clarinet player and the ex-owner of a vegetarian restaurant in Greenwich Village. When he went into hospital for a simple operation on an ulcer, he never returned to consciousness. The operation was a total success, but the same could not be said for the anaesthesia; Miles had to be put into hibernation in the hope that technological progress would allow doctors to deal with the problem in the future. The scientists inform the new arrival about the politics of their times. The ruler is the Great Leader, who shows himself only on television, in white clothes, alongside his dog, on a resplendent cliff. The scientists who have thawed Miles out are on the side of the rebels, who want to overthrow the tyrant, and they ask him to join them. As a citizen of the past no contemporary records of him exist at all, and therefore he is free to act incognito. His reaction to this proposal is very, very lukewarm, but before any decision can be taken, the place is raided by the police. The only one who manages to get away is Miles. He ends up in a van which is carrying robot domestic servants, he disguises himself as one of them and takes refuge in the house of a poetess called Luna (Diane Keaton), whose vanity is only equalled by her lack of talent. After a party for intellectuals, during which the fake robot has to make a pudding (which grows

Cryogenised in 1973 and thawed out in 2173, Miles
Monroe (Woody Allen) swings from a magnetic tape
while attempting to steal the nose of the Great Leader.

to giant size and has to be beaten
down with a broom), and after a
riotous escape from the robot factory
(where he ran the risk of having his
head screwed off), Miles escapes
again, taking Luna with him. They
wander through the woods, living on
giant vegetables they have stolen from
a futuristic cultivator. They narrowly
escape being caught by the police and
Luna realises to her horror that the
guards are shooting at her as well,
without taking into consideration the
fact that she is a political conformist.
In the end, they find themselves back
at the starting point, at the scientist's
house where Miles had been reawakened. They have an idyllic dinner together, after which the police come back
again and this time Miles is taken prisoner, while Luna manages to escape.

Instead of sacrificing the 'alien', the
authorities decide to reprogramme
him. They give him a brainwash, new
clothes, his own apartment and even
an electronic pet dog. Miles would
have remained a model citizen, but for
the reappearance of the poetess who
has since become a fervent subversive.
She had hidden herself in the forest,
and after struggling there for survival
against natural hazards, she had
finally reached the camp of the revolutionaries. Here she has developed a
passion for their muscular leader,
Erno. She returns in secret to recon-
vert Miles to the cause, and finds
herself having to struggle against his
new character as a perfectly integrated
member of society. So the twentieth
century man is made to undergo the
whole process again, and his brain
received another series of stimuli to
get it back to the way it was before.
After living through, in the form of
psychodrama, a lunch at his parents'
house and a scene from A Streetcar
Named Desire, Miles is back on form

Fleeing from the police who have raided the house of the scientists who thawed him out, Miles attempts to balance on a ladder which is too short.

and ready for a most important task. Accompanied by Luna, with whom he never ceases a jealous bickering, he infiltrates the enemy headquarters. There he discovers that an attempt has been made on the Great Leader's life and that the only part of him left alive is his nose. The government wants to clone it, to put it through a process of cell replication, so that from the nose the rest of the body can be reconstructed and the Great Leader brought back to life. Disguised as doctors, Miles and Luna hurry off to try and sabotage the project, and eventually they succeed in throwing the nose under a steamroller. With their mission accomplished, the couple are reunited. The handsome Erno is forgotten, even though he is to be the new Great Leader. 'Political solution's don't work', declares Miles sententiously. So what does he believe in. 'In sex and death' he answers. 'Except that after death you don't get nausea.'

'I'd like to be a graceful physical comedian', Woody Allen had declared a year before he made this film. And he added: 'Because of the nature of Chaplin's background and Keaton's background, they came to the screen with a tremendous training in acrobatics. There's nothing in my background that's like that. . . . I would like to develop into a better physical comedian. I think that I have the instincts, but not the grace to do it.'

Sleeper is without doubt his most coherent and determined attempt at classical comedy. It is full of situations comparable to those that his great predecessors made use of in the early years of this century: chases, disguises, struggles against inanimate objects. At one moment, Woody is left suspended over a void, hanging onto a magnetic tape – we think of Harold Lloyd; he paints his face white – we are reminded of Harry Langdon; he eats to the sound of music – this is Chaplin shaving to the rhythm of the czardas in *The Great Dictator*; he tries to keep his balance on a ladder that is too short – here is Keaton again. And, for sure, Italian audiences are going to recall the great Toto when Miles dresses up like a domestic robot and moves like a puppet. It is a notable fact that *Sleeper* is the only film in which Allen adopts the masks of a clown: he dresses up right through the film, from flying man, complete with a micro-helicopter, to pneumatic man. The results are often wonderful, but the effort is always apparent. In all

(Below) Disguised as a robot, Miles struggles with a pudding that has gone crazy.
(Right) Taken back to the factory for a check-up, he runs the risk of having his head screwed off and replaced by a better looking one.

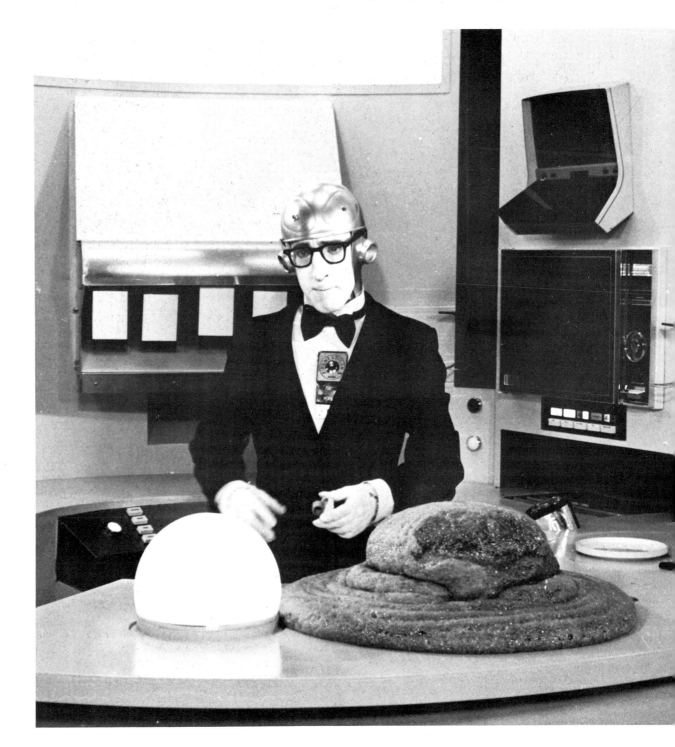

revivals, there is in part a self-consciousness and a premeditation, which takes away much of the freshness and gaiety of the inspiration. Nevertheless, in spite of the numerous ideas he borrows from his great predecessors, Allen always remains himself, even as an actor. This is less the case in his mimic style, which is uneven and does not stand up to comparison with that of the originals, than it is in the personality of the character he portrays and in his quick-fire verbal inventions. It is not by chance that from *Sleeper* onwards, pure comedy occupies a less important part in Allen's films. Very probably, this was an enlightening experiment: the custard pie-in-the-face formula could not work with an actor whose main strength lay in his command of language. Two of the sequences previously mentioned go to prove this, and from the point of view of mime they are probably the best in the film. In the first, Miles escapes from a ledge by means of a ladder which turns out to be too short; in the other, he eats to the rhythm of music in a playful attempt to impress Luna. But in both these instances, Allen has to have recourse to film editing, both to prolong the length of time he is balancing on top of the ladder, and to keep up the rhythm during the meal (there he also makes use of speeded up shots). These are two successful moments in the film, but the great comedians of earlier days would have accomplished it all without trick photography, and they would have felt they were cheating otherwise.

The interplay between the comic (Woody Allen) and the 'stooge' (Diane Keaton) works perfectly. The actress has nothing of the clown about her and makes no attempt to become one. On those rare occasions when she does resort to clowning, the audience tends to feel sorry for her (as when she grabs for a trailing vine in imitation of Tarzan, or draws a bow and the bowstring hits her in the face). But Diane, witty in her heedlessness, delicate in her moments, is a perfect foil to ever-fidgety Woody Allen. Miles and Luna are the only two fully rounded characters in the film. The others are deprived of their identity by their very roles (the policemen), or are confined

The uneven struggle with the mega-vegetables produced by the futuristic cultivators of the twenty-second century.

to brief, sporadic appearances. Of course, it would have been impossible to dwell on other characters, without being forced to provide a more general description of the world of the future which, throughout the film, is portrayed as rather frightening. The essence of the comedy here stems from the upside-down perspective of Miles, a man of our times projected two hundred years into the future. His behaviour and his witticisms are especially funny when he makes reference to the past. 'Every time he left the White House the secret service counted the silver', Miles recounts, in an attempt to describe Nixon to people of the twenty second century; 'I go into hospital for a minor operation and find myself two thousand months behind in my rent', he mutters as soon as he is brought out of hibernation.

What kind of future does Woody Allen foresee? Although he only traces an outline, it is far from reassuring, not too dissimilar to the contra-utopias of Huxley or Orwell. A dictatorship, propped up by a faultless, technocratic organisation, controls the world. Menacing security police are constantly on patrol (that they turn out in the end to be morons like the Keystone Cops is pure chance); cold buildings shelter the humans; the only joys of life are the drug-ball and the orgasmatron, the orgasm machine. The cinemagoer begins to look for a reaction against so much dreariness, and bit by bit the film turns into a familiar adventure story: the good guys will beat the bad guys, thanks to the assistance of the clumsy stranger, promoted to the rank of hero. But it doesn't go exactly like that, and Sleeper becomes very pessimistic. Miles, a peaceful middle class man transported out of his own times, has

absolutely no ties to the cause of the revolution. He is dragged into it, he fights and he wins; but always he has mental reservations: in reality, it all has nothing to do with him. With the tyranny overthrown, his final comment is the same as in Bananas: the new leader will not be any better than the previous one. It is not for nothing that the final scene takes the form of a tête-à-tête, in a white and sterile room. Miles has simply succeeded in extracting himself from his anxieties: at last he can devote his attention to the things that interest him; his private life, the girl who loves him, sex. So what if death drops by sooner or later?

Composed and filmed with care, very well served by the designs and the special effects, Sleeper was very well received. But in fact it has certain defects, particularly in the structure. Nor is his problem with the plot resolved this time either. For sure, Woody Allen has passed the stage of assembling a myriad of independent ideas and scenes. All in all, the plot is solid and well developed. But the problem, in comedy films, is in finding the right mixture between the burlesque elements and the narrative. The gags and witticisms must not interrupt the action. Buster Keaton, who had an obsession about not boring the audience, often talked about having to cut an excellent scene from The Navigator, just because he was loathe to slow down the course of the action.

In Sleeper, on the other hand, this is exactly what happens. One situation rarely leads to another, and so the sequences often appear as digressions. The thread of events is mostly 'spoken' in the dialogues and even though everyone runs around, very agitated, in a cinematographic sense

Luna (Diane Keaton) and Miles in the operating-theatre which has been prepared for the cloning of the Great Leader's nose.

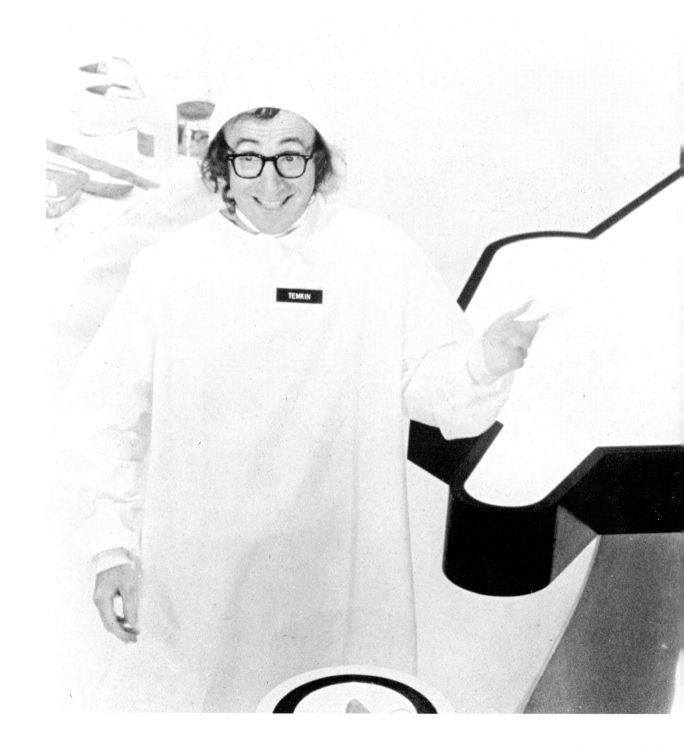

very little action takes place.

We should conclude with an observation on the music. Irrepressible New Orleans Jazz, very much from the 19th century, is the bizarre accompaniment to the action in 2173. The music is composed and played by Woody Allen himself, who went to New Orleans to join the Preservation Hall Jazz Band for the occasion. Some of the critics did not like this choice. Woody answered: 'It would have been old-time and obvious and not inventive to use the same silly science fiction music used by everyone for *Sleeper*. Also it was the music one heard in old, silent comedies which *Sleeper* was modelled after. It was the most perfect music possible and did everything I wanted it to do.'

Love And Death

Setting: The Russia of the early years of the last century (precise dates: between 1805, the Battle of Austerlitz, and 1812, the Napoleonic campaign in Russia). The film begins in flashback. 'It's incredible,' says the off screen voice of Boris Grusenko (Woody Allen), while swirls of cloud chase each other across the screen. 'I'm going to be executed for a crime I didn't commit. Tomorrow morning at six. I was supposed to be executed at five, but I've got a good lawyer: he got me clemency.'

The condemned man then remembers his childhood. His father owned a small piece of land (so small that he kept it in his pocket), his strong, extrovert brothers, his own mystic visions. Also dating back to this period are his first conversations with Death, a spectral figure carrying a scythe, which inspires him with both fear and fascination at the same time. Then, when he is grown up, he meets his beautiful cousin, Sonia (Diane Keaton), and his passions are aroused, but his love in unrequited for she has given her heart to his brother, Ivan. Finally the war. Napoleon invades Austria. With enthusiasm, the Russians prepare to fight. Only Boris is reluctant. In fact, he proclaims himself a 'militant coward'; but that does not excuse him from putting on a uniform and undergoing training. Three days before leaving for the front, he is granted leave, and makes use of it to go and visit his relatives in St. Petersburg. That evening he goes to the opera to see Mozart's The Magic Flute. *He meets the Countess Alexandrovna (Olga Georges-Picot), a nymphomaniac, who takes a fancy to him. But his most important meeting is with Sonia, his old love. She is now married to a herring merchant, but it was a marriage entered into out*

Russia, at the beginning of the nineteenth century: two tête-à-têtes between Boris (Woody Allen) and Sonia (Diane Keaton).

of spite because Ivan had chosen another. Sonia is unhappy, and she drowns her unhappiness in a multitude of affairs; but for Boris there is no room in her heart. He goes off to war. Dead and wounded, explosions, guns as far as the eye can see. Boris ends up taking refuge in the mouth of a cannon, from which he is shot out like a cannon ball. Fate causes him to land on a gathering of enemy officers and he blows them up. He receives honours and medals. Sonia, recently widowed (the herring merchant has been killed while trying to defend his wife's sullied honour in a duel), now also has another terrible blow to bear: the loss of Ivan as well, who has died in battle. Boris Grusenko comes home to a hero's welcome. Again he meets the Countess Alexandrovna, and he passes the night with her. But her jealous lover, Lebedkov (Harold Gould), wants revenge. He challenges Boris to a duel, and Boris, who is a terrible shot with a pistol, goes off to cry on Sonia's shoulder. Moved to compassion, she promises to marry him if he comes out of it alive. Against all the odds, that is just what happens: and the amazed girl has to keep her promise. Nevertheless their marriage turns out to be happy and full of joy, only marred by an occasional fit of nervous depression for Boris (who continues to be prone to extraordinary visions), and by financial prob-

97

lems (but Sonia is the perfect house-wife and becomes very good at cooking snow, which is cheap). Then, unfortunately, Napoleon returns to the scene. This time it is Sonia who is inflamed: she and Boris will kill the invader and free the world from his bloodstained ambitions. As usual, the unfortunate Boris protests, but in the end he has to give in. They go to the palace, pretending to be Don Francisco of Spain and his sister (whom they have previously removed from the scene), and the couple succeed in luring the emperor into Sonia's bedroom. Boris is on the point of pulling the trigger when someone else commits the murder. What is more, the victim is not Napoleon, but his double. Nonetheless, Boris is condemned to death. We see him meditating in his cell, and we are back to the opening scene. Suddenly, an angel appears to him and announces: 'You will not be executed.' Boris is exultant, but the angel is lying! Sonia is prattling to a cousin, when she sees her loved one with Death, enveloped

(Left) Boris' father (Zvee Scooler) owned a small piece
of land. He kept it in his pocket.
(Below) Sonia, the unfaithful wife of a herring merchant,
in the arms of one of her lovers.

*in a white shroud. 'What's it like,
being dead?' she asks. 'You know the
chicken at Treskie's restaurant? Well,
it's worse.' The final scene sees Boris
and Death both dancing away along a
tree lined avenue. They disappear into
the distance.*

Boris, a soldier in spite of himself, is compelled to take part in the training, but he is incapable of even drawing his sword.

Sleeper was set in the future, *Love And Death* is set in the past. Counting *Everything You Always Wanted To Know About Sex* as well, it is the third film in a row which has a fantasy environment, far removed from the urban realities of the cement-filled world which lies at the origins of Woody's character. This real world, which is probably too complex to be reduced to the caricatures of cinema comedy, comes back in the films from this lifelong New Yorker which follow. But, though exotic, the settings are not from a folk tale. Allen is not Bob Hope, ever ready to take up a *Road To...* and surround his 'numbers' with motley costumes from enchanting countries all over the world. The Russia of *Love And Death* corresponds perfectly to the temperament of Woody Allen. It forms part of his voyage of return to Europe: the Europe of films, the Europe of books, the Europe of his own ancestors. This film is also a tribute paid to the spiritual roots of the New York Jews, just as the role of the *Inspector General* after Gogol had been for Danny Kaye, and the directing of *The Twelve*

The death of the herring salesman allows Sonia to get married to Boris. Times are hard and cold: she becomes expert at cooking snow.

Chairs had been for Mel Brooks. The Russia of Woody Allen is mainly literary. It is modelled on the Tolstoy of *War And Peace*, but characters are also made up from odds and ends of other Russian novels. Boris is a mixture of Tolstoy's Pierre Bezukhov and Andrei Belkonsky, while his name is the male version of Dostoyevsky's Grusenka. The dialogue, characters and plot are a treat for Slavists. The obsession with wheat, which is expressed in two conversations, bring to mind Levin in *Anna Karenina*. The repetitive metaphysical dialogues recall the works of Dostoyevsky, while the execution episode comes from his biography. There is Sonais' flippant remark. 'I am half saint and half whore', surprisingly similar to the judgment made by Zdanov about Anna Akmatova. And finally, in prison between Boris and his father, there is a dialogue made up of the titles of Russian novels.

But it should not be forgotten that New York is also well represented. Even before the pictures of the nineteenth century Slavid world appear on the screen, the voice of Woody Allen

Count Lebedkov (Harold Gould) puts his hand to his heart. Contrary to all expectations, the duel has not proved fatal for Boris.

can be heard off screen: speaking with a broad Brooklyn accent. The whole film flows along a double track, on the one hand respecting the historical conventions of the plot, and on the other completely distorting them. For example, Allen does not hesitate to interrupt the action to address himself directly to the audience (in this film the 'camera-look' becomes almost habitual). As he did in *Sleeper*, only more insistently, he uses a humorous device of anachronism (modern eyeglasses, a popcorn vendor at the battle of Austerlitz, boxing gloves for the erotic match with Sonia). For cinema history buffs he continues to offer a multiplicity of citations: Eisenstein, Bergman. . . . The mental landscape is still that of a victim of urban post-industrial neurosis. 'I have learned that human beings are split in two: mind and body. The mind embraces the most noble aspirations, like poetry or philosophy. But it is the body which enjoys itself. . . . If it turns out that there is a God, I don't think he will be bad. I think the worst thing that could be said about him is that he is an underachiever. After all, there are worse things than death. If you've ever spent an evening with an insurance salesman, then you'll know what I'm talking about . . . I think the secret is this: don't think that 'death is the end', instead think of it as an excellent way of cutting your expenses. As for love . . . it is not the 'quantity' of your sexual acts which counts, it is the 'quality'. However, if the quantity is less than once every seven-eight months, then I would have myself checked over by a doctor. Well, that's all folks.' This is the final admonition that Boris-Woody gives to his audience. We remain in the realm of insecurity, of fear exorcised with irony, or obsession with love and the

end, of sex and death. Even if the character is a contemporary of Napoleon and moves around in St. Petersburg, he remains the maladjusted neurotic we know so well. Transposing him to a very different setting is a favourite dramatic device: some poor devil is set down in an environment with which he is completely out of tune, the better to make him stand out and excite the audiences' laughter.

Love and Death brings together all the comic procedures perfected by Allen in his preceding films. First of all there are the references to other films. From Eisenstein: a lively seduction scene is accompanied by the music composed by Prokofiev for the battle in *Alexander Nevsky*. In the course of a similar scene, we see the three famous lions from *Battleship Potemkin* (couchant, gardant, rampant), but the third has been replaced by one which is worn out by its sexual activities. During the battle of Austerlitz, there is a close-up of a soldier wounded in the eye (*Potemkin* again, from the Odessa steps). From Bergman comes Death bearing a scythe, similar to the one in *The Seventh Seal*, and certain close-ups, in which a profile is crossed with a full face shot, seem to be taken from *Persona*. From Chaplin comes the scene where Boris is wandering around a cannon, recalling the hero of *The Great Dictator* alongside Big Bertha. And on closer inspection, there is also Miklos Jancso, Bob Hope, and who knows who else. It is also worth mentioning a superb example of the 'throwaway' technique, in perhaps the best scene from the film. In the foreground, a Napoleonic general speaks of his far-fetched plans for the future, while in the background, out of focus, the emperor and his double are seen walking about,

and then they start fighting each other like squabbling street urchins. This is an effect taken from the handbook: the 'verbal comedy' from a motionless character is added to the 'visual comedy' of two silent characters. As for the 'camera-look', we have already mentioned its frequent use. Allen shows himself to be a master of it, not only as an actor in the quality of his performance, but also as a director, in his recourse to it at the right times. Thus, at the dramatic moment when

Boris is getting ready to shoot Napoleon, the interminable monologue into which he launches himself only serves to increase the suspense. Another interesting aspect is that Allen makes use again, in a very effective way, of certain typical elements from his own comic repertoire. Just as, in some of his previous films, he had made use more than once of titanic struggles with inanimate objects, and the nail-biting anxieties of preparing for a romantic appointment, in *Love And*

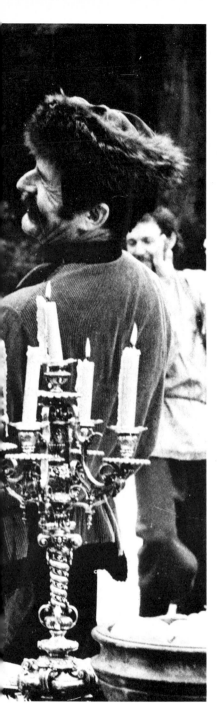

Two aspects of Tsarist Russia: peasants making merry
and the pomp of the great palaces.

(Below) During his married life with
Sonia, Boris devotes himself to
writing poetry.
(Right) Dining with Napoleon
(James Tolkan, in the middle between
Diane Keaton and Woody Allen),
before the attempt on his life.

Death he refuses certain original ideas
from some of his other films. For
example: the sergeant in the Russian
army is, surprise, surprise, black; c.f.
the black sperm in *Everything You
Always Wanted To Know About Sex*.
But, above all, he reutilises entire passages, revised and corrected. Mimed
seduction from a distance (here between Boris and the countess, in
Bananas between Fielding and the
beautiful guerilla, in *Sleeper* between
Miles and Luna); an execution with
humorous consequences (also in
Casino Royale and in *Bananas*); mili-
tary training (*Bananas* again). One
can say that Allen has achieved a
certain maturity which means that he
no longer has to focus on his own
personality and style. Instead, con-
scious of the depth of his own creative
background, he can now draw from it,
adapt it and make use of it as he needs
to.

In fact, *Love And Death* is a
mature, well-made film. His skill in
directing, while still not masterful, is
sure and efficient, without jokes which
fall flat or amateurisms. The focussing
is harmonious and functional, the
camera moves about smoothly, the
editing maintains a good rhythm.
Even the directing holds together.
Again Allen creates a whirlpool of
events and digressions, but this time
he manages to keep the subordinate to
the development of the story.

Another sign of maturity is the
perfect interpretation of Diane
Keaton, as a proper 'heroine' and not

just a supporting player. This had been a problem of considerable importance. Allen's world was that of an isolated person, in which another presence was absolutely superfluous. On the other hand, the absence of real human relations and the continual presence of Allen alone on the screen, sometimes created a cumbersome effect. As 'different' as Woody, although in another way, Diane interacts well with him. She has enough intelligence and sense of proportion to

know how to be funny without clowning, nor affectation, and she does not steal the scenes from her partner.

The sixth (counting *Play It Again, Sam*) and final work of Allen's first film-making period, *Love And Death* marks a turning point. In a cinematographic sense, it is his most successful work, the summation of bright, original ideas and intuitions gathered up in the course of years of effort. But can we really speak of it as a monument

The failure of the attempt on Napoleon's life leads Boris into prison, and then before a firing squad.

of the comic cinema? The answer is doubtful. The truly memorable sequence, the scene which would always feature in the anthologies, like Buster Keaton's flight before the blocks of stone, or Harpo Marx's duel with the lemonade seller, seems once again to escape Woody Allen. As a film comedian Woody Allen seems to be blessed with great ability, but not with genius. Against this, the film puts heavy emphasis on 'serious' themes: love, death, the after life, the torments of doubt, and, above all, the possibility of establishing a warm dialogue with other human beings. Boris is the first of Allen's characters to be shown in a stable relationship with someone. In spite of all the declarations of passionate love, with Sonia he establishes a solid raport, but again not a relationship based on tenderness. This will be the theme of *Annie Hall* and *Manhattan*.

Annie Hall

The film opens with a close-up of
Woody Allen, who addresses the audience as in a night club monologue:
'There's an old joke. Two elderly
women are at a Catskills mountain
resort, and one of them says: "Boy,
the food at this place is really
terrible." The other one says: "Yeah. I
know, and such . . . small portions."
Well, that's essentially how I feel
about life. Full of loneliness and
misery and suffering and unhappiness,
and it's all over much too quickly. The
other important joke for me is the one
that's usually attributed to Groucho
Marx, but I think it appears originally
in Freud's Wit And Its Relation To
The Unconscious. And it goes like this
(I'm paraphrasing): "I would never
wanna belong to any club that would
have someone like me for a member."
That's the key joke of my adult life in
terms of my relationship with
women.' The monologue continues;
he has reached his fortieth birthday
with the risk of a crisis in his life, in
the light of approaching old age, and
his newly broken off relationship with
Annie, which is still incomprehensible
to him.

   The author of this impassioned self-
analysis is the hero of the film, Alvy
Singer. He is an established comedian,
well regarded, but constantly plagued
by self doubts. As a child, he fell into a
depression when he discovered that
the universe is expanding, and that in
a few billion years the Earth will be
reduced to dust. The family doctor
brought him round with the only
argument possible: 'We've gotta try to
enjoy ourselves while we're here.' At
six years of age, he formed his first
passion for the opposite sex: in class,
he kissed the girl beside him, who
turned away with a grimace of
distaste, and he was told off by the
teacher as a precocious satyr.

Annie Hall (Diane Keaton) and Alvy Singer (Woody Allen) and their reciprocal courtship.

In adult life, he has been married twice before beginning his famous relationship with Annie. His first wife, Allison, was Jewish like himself. They met at a gala in support of Adlai Stevenson, the Democratic Presidential Candidate who was defeated by Eisenhower. They were divorced after the assassination of John Kennedy, when in their bedroom she accused him of talking about conspiracies and crime just to avoid making love. His second wife, Robin, is tense, nervous and incapable of thinking about anything else apart from her imaginary illnesses and her surprise parties for the city's intellectuals. Then Annie came along. One day, Alvy's best friend, Rob, and his girl-friend, had brought along this provincial girl from Chippewa Falls, Wisconsin, for a game of doubles at tennis. Afterwards, half laughing, half apprehensive, she had invited Alvy back to her house, and they courted each other with stock phrases (complete with subtitles to let us know what they were really thinking of each other). It was a great love, the kind that leaves its mark forever. Alvy Singer felt he had to play the role of a Pygmalion: he bought her books, he urged her to enroll in university courses, he started her on psychoanalysis.

And, naturally, he encouraged her during her first appearances as a singer. In many ways, Annie was a perfect partner for Alvy, but she was not an easy person to get along with. Unsure of herself, indecisive, with a tendency towards frigidity, her moods alternated constantly, up and down. Her spontaneity compensates for his more reserved affection ('You don't really like emotions, do you?'), and yet when she suggests that they live together she scares him, and puts him on the defensive. Her parents, the

111

(Below) A voyage down memory lane: Alvy, with his friend Rob (Tony Roberts) and Annie, visits the school he went to as a child.
(Right) The same group at a cocktail party.

Halls, are classic WASPS, white Anglo-Saxon Protestants. They have a poor opinion of Jews like Alvy, who also happens to be very sensitive on this point. They have very strict and formal table manners, the opposite of the Singers, who are unceremonious and noisy.

A banal scene of jealousy leads to their first separation. Alvy finds himself a partner for the night, a rock music journalist, who tells him, 'Sex with you is really a Kafka-esque experience', but at three o'clock in the morning he rushes back to Annie as soon as she calls him to come and remove a spider. They are reconciled. But their relationship is compromised. On a split-screen we see in parallel their sessions with the psychoanalyst. To the question, 'How often do you have sexual relations?', he answers with a disconsolate, 'Hardly ever . . . maybe three times a week', while she sighs, 'Constantly. I'd say three times a week.'

Matters come to a head when Alvy is called out to California to take part in a television show. California is hell on earth for the neurotic New York Jew accustomed to his books, to stress, to thick fog, and cold winters. California is sun-kissed. Everything seems easy and natural. People think only of superficial pleasures, and their words seem hollow. But what is worse is that in California there is a record producer who has set his eyes on Annie, and who makes her attractive proposals. On their return flight to New York it is now clear that the couple feel the need for a complete separation. It is a bad moment to get over but, as he says, they face up to it 'with maturity'. They divide the books, they argue a bit, but everything seems to be sorted out.

But it is not. With a few months gone by, Alvy begins to realise that he is missing Annie. The girl is now living in Los Angeles, with the record producer. He calls her up on the phone, then he gets on a plane and goes to look for her. She refuses categorically to go back with him. Alvy is so upset that he is unable even to drive. He tears up his licence under the nose of the policeman who is questioning him and he even ends up in prison. It is his old friend Rob, the one who had introduced him to Annie and who is now working in Los Angeles, who pays his bail and gets him set free again. Rob has become a true Californian: for driving he wears an elaborate white suit with a hood, which

(Left) Reality (Annie makes her debut as a singer), and a memory (Alvy at one of his first shows as a stand-up comic).
(Below) Alvy at the tennis game during which he meets Annie.

'keeps away the alpha rays, and stops you from getting old.'

Alvy takes up his old, everyday life and begins to write a comedy, a theatrical version of his affair with Annie Hall. Except that his comedy has a happy ending: at the bar in California, where he has gone to meet up with her, after the reproaches and sulks are over, a kiss puts the seal on their reunion. This is really also the finale of the film, because in reality their relationship is not ended. It is simply changed. Annie returns to New York, she sees her ex-lover again, they chatter and laugh together. They have become friends. And so, concludes the off screen voice of Alvy in his monologue again, 'I remember an old joke, you know, the one about the guy who goes to the psychiatrist and says to him: "Doctor, my brother is mad. He thinks he's a chicken!" And the doctor replied: "Why don't you bring him here to me?" And the young man says: "I would, but I need the eggs". Well, I'd say that's more or less what I think about human relationships. They are totally irrational, mad and absurd . . . but I think that we will go on looking for them because the majority of us need the eggs'.

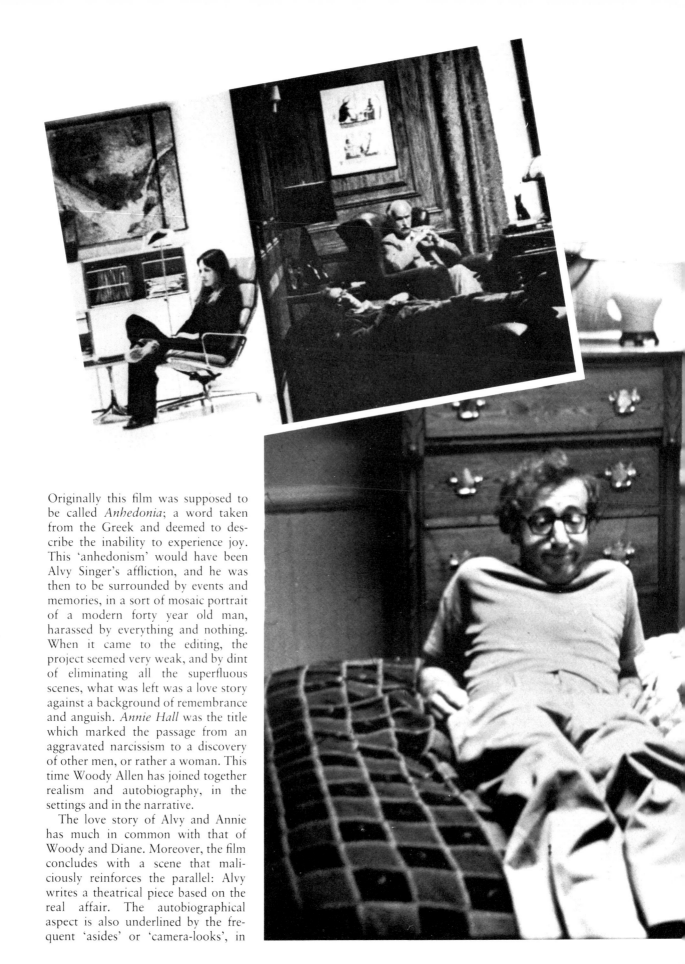

Originally this film was supposed to be called *Anhedonia*; a word taken from the Greek and deemed to describe the inability to experience joy. This 'anhedonism' would have been Alvy Singer's affliction, and he was then to be surrounded by events and memories, in a sort of mosaic portrait of a modern forty year old man, harassed by everything and nothing. When it came to the editing, the project seemed very weak, and by dint of eliminating all the superfluous scenes, what was left was a love story against a background of remembrance and anguish. *Annie Hall* was the title which marked the passage from an aggravated narcissism to a discovery of other men, or rather a woman. This time Woody Allen has joined together realism and autobiography, in the settings and in the narrative.

The love story of Alvy and Annie has much in common with that of Woody and Diane. Moreover, the film concludes with a scene that maliciously reinforces the parallel: Alvy writes a theatrical piece based on the real affair. The autobiographical aspect is also underlined by the frequent 'asides' or 'camera-looks', in

The split-screen during the sessions at the
psychoanalyst, on the subject of their intimate lives.
'How often do you make love?'
Her: 'All the time! At least three times a week!'
Him: 'Hardly ever . . . perhaps three times a week.'

which the actor addresses himself
directly to the camera (i.e. the audience) to tell a story or comment on
what is happening. Caught up by a
passion for confession, Woody Allen
does not recoil from exposing the less
sympathetic aspects of his character,
his egocentricity, the presumption
with which he attempts to shape
Annie's mind and impose his ideas on
her. If Alvy Singer doesn't become an
out and out irritation, this can only be
for two reasons. Firstly, Alvy often
acts as the 'shadow' for Annie, like
a dark background against which the
young woman's brightness stands out,
and this helps us to see him in a more
attractive light. Secondly, his constant
appeal to the spectators, taken into his
confidence from the very first frame,
creates another relationship with the
audience this time; and they end up
feeling indulgent towards the haun-
ting, haunted windbag. This was not
to be the case in *Stardust Memories*,
where a very similar character, Sandy
Bates, is the only pivot for all the
action and ends up seeming
unbearable.

Why does Alvy Singer fall in love
with Annie Hall? Because she is a
WASP while he is Jewish, of course;
she is pretty, she gives him the chance
to play macho games, with his books
and his intellect; because she gives
herself over to him like clay to be
modelled, and he feels within himself
the arrogant urge to be Pygmalion.
Most of all, as observed by Serge
Daney in *Cahiers Du Cinema*, because
she competes with him right from the
start. She refuses to allow him the
dominion of the 'word'. The whole
universe seems to exist only as a reflec-
tion of Alvy Singer: men, women,
circumstances, memories, all lay down
before his intellectual and verbal
superiority; the first and last words

117

are always his; and words are his instrument for dominating the present, the past, other people, and himself. Except for Annie Hall. Annie courts him even while he is courting her, she imposes her own odd way of thinking on Alvy, even while accepting his advice, she dresses so casually that she appears eccentric even to him, who is a veteran of casual dress. Contrary to the way it might seem, their love does not end at the moment when the creature is grown up and can abandon the creator. In reality, the relationship between Alvy and Annie has been on an equal footing right from the start, and it continues to be so even at the end when the couple have become good friends. Their relationship draws strength from the game of reciprocal seduction, it is sometimes a matter of conceding and sometimes a matter of winning supremacy over each other. It is not by chance that Alvy grasps at words to set his heart at ease: writing a comedy for the theatre is an act of mastery over his life. It gives back to the writer his lost power.

In *Annie Hall* are some of the most subtle moments from Woody Allen's films. Just think of the spider hunt, of the hilarious struggle with the lobsters, the walk along the beach when Annie tells Alvy about her previous loves. The whole story of their relationship is told with a well-balanced sweetness, which is rare and maybe unique in modern American cinema. Maybe love doesn't triumph over death (it is curious how this theme is present here as much as it was in the film entitled *Love And Death*), but it gives it a good fight. If Alvy was not sure that the universe is expanding, if he did not buy so many books with the word 'death' in the title, if he was not aware that, in spite

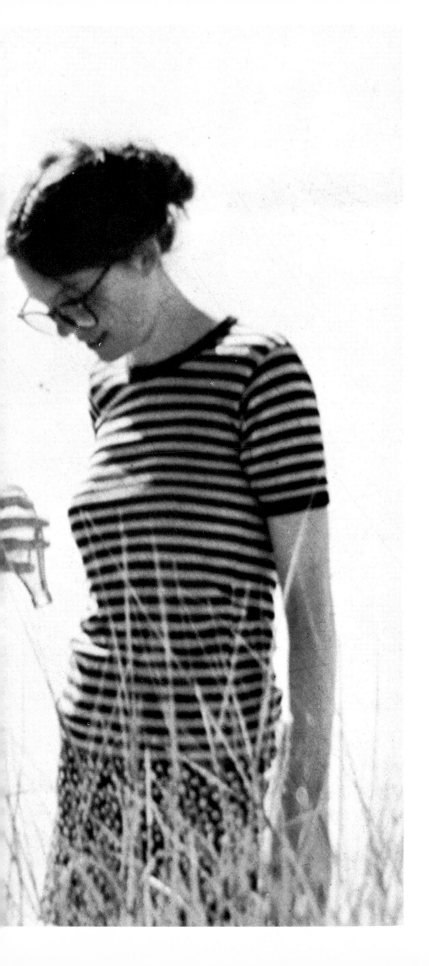

of all his intellectual games, he was going to end up dying, he would be singing out about the triumph of love and he would leave the anhedonia to the dictionary. Basically, this is the message to be distilled from the three jokes at the beginning and the end of the film. Above all, it is the last joke which remains more easily engraved on the memory and so appears to be the most important: remember, 'the majority of us need the eggs.'

The great secret of the success of *Annie Hall* lies both in the screenplay, which is secure because the dialogue is excellent and the characters are well defined, and also in the editing. A complicated but harmonious device is used, of overlapping so that flashback succeeds flashback, recounting all the digressions in the story and the various developments of the theme in a way that is lucid although it is fragmented. As for the rest, from the highly praised use of the split-screen (the screen divided into two, showing two simultaneous actions), to the subtitles and the animated cartoons, it is probably more cosmetic than of any great substance. As has been mentioned elsewhere, *Annie Hall* ends the sequence of caricature films made by Allen and inaugurates the era of the films of observation. Practically the only things that keep this film tied to the world of comedy are the flood of jokes (which come thick and fast) and certain situations (especially the paradoxical dialogues that Alvy has with passers-by, who seem to be completely *au fait* with the events that Alvy discusses with them). In everything else, this is an intimate and often grievous drama.

The accumulation of stylistic and linguistic flourishes displayed this time by Woody Allen stop him from going over the top in cinematographic cita-

(Below) Alvy in prison for reckless driving after his final
break-up with Annie.
(Right) With the journalist (Shelley Duvall), who says to
Alvy: 'Sex with you is a Kafka-esque experience.'

tions. If Alvy chooses to go and see *Face To Face* by Ingmar Bergman and *The Sorrow And The Pity* by Marcel Ophuls, this is mainly because of an intellectual temperament which sees him as particularly sensitive to anti-semitism.

The other allusions are more veiled. An amusing sequence (although not very effective in the long run because the great personality acts so badly) is the intrusion of Marshall McLuhan who, to Alvy's great delight, tells off a loud mouthed little professor who distorts his own point of view on mass communication. Finally, *Annie Hall* also has the merit of being excellently filmed. Grey in the outdoor New York scenes, dazzling in the Californian sunlight, golden for Alvy's memories of childhood. It is the achievement of Gordon Willis, working for the first time with Woody Allen, but his contribution is already shown to be valuable and he adds much to the success of the film.

121

Interiors

A wealthy New York family. The parents are called Eve and Arthur, the three daughters, Renata, Joey and Flyn. They are at the stage where parental care and attention is at an end: Renata is about to be married to a writer, Joey is living with a politically active young man, and Flyn, working as an actress, travels constantly. Freed from his obligations as a father, Arthur asks for a 'trial' separation from his wife. Suddenly all is drama. Eve sees the world she has so carefully built up falling apart around her, and she plunges into a long depression. The film develops along the path of Eve's attempts to regain her own mental balance, in order to reach a relationship with her husband again. We also focus on the interplay of the characters as expressed in the daughters' lengthy conversations between each other, with Eve, with their father and with their companions. Renata is a successful poet, while her husband is an unsuccessful novelist. A silent conflict arising from envy and jealousy undermines their relationship. Joey is unable to find the right career and suffers more than the others because of the lack of understanding between her parents. She dedicates a great deal of her time to her mother, and cannot resign herself to the fact that she is unloved and that Eve prefers Renata. Very absorbed in her films, and in drugs, Flyn is seldom around. For her part, Eve forces herself to carry on with her job as an interior decorator. Her choices and her dominating personality influence the lives of all those around her. And finally, along comes Pearl. She is a woman of about sixty, but very young for her age, jovial and open minded, who loves life as a physical fact. She is the new wife-to-be of Arthur, who now forces Eve into a divorce. On the evening of the celebration of the new marriage, Eve returns to the house by the sea which was hers and where her rival is now installed. She has an argument with Joey, and they are totally unable to communicate with each other. Finally, Eve walks off towards the beach and disappears into the ocean. Joey follows her and, in an effort to rescue her, she in turn puts herself in danger of drowning. She is saved by her boyfriend and by Pearl. The film ends with the three sisters staring out at the ocean after having put flowers on their mother's coffin.

That Woody Allen was on the verge of making a dramatic film, after so many years in the ranks of comedy, was evident and even declared ('When you do comedy you're not sitting at the grown-ups' table, you're sitting at the childrens' table'). Perhaps it would be more exact to say that this is the first occasion on which he was not afraid not to be funny. Few smiles and no laughs lighten this brooding story of fashionable 'interiors' (the title alludes to the double meaning of the word: interior and internal). To make such an uncommercial film as this, after all the laurels and the box-office success of *Annie Hall*, smacks of masochism. But, all in all, the film definitely has a certain value, even if it resembles a film by Bergman. And we can take advantage of *Interiors* to once and for all settle the question of Bergman's influence which has irritated so many critics. That it exists is beyond doubt. There are even a couple of moments (the memories of the family when the girls were young, the dialogue between Joey and the mother who is about to commit suicide) in which the similarities between this film and *Autumn Sonata* are amazing; all the

Two of the three sisters with their mother. From the left:
Joey (Mary Beth Hurt), Renata (Diane Keaton), and
Eve (Geraldine Page).

(Below) Frederick (Richard Jordan), Renata's husband, and Mike (Sam Waterston), Joey's companion.
(Right) Arthur (E. G. Marshall), the father, with his second wife Pearl (Maureen Stapleton).

more so if we consider that they were both made at almost the same time and so neither one could have copied from the other. But before we ask where and why Allen is different from Bergman, it is worth pointing out that the value of an artist is not lessened just because his style is influenced by the style of others. If this was the case, then all those who are grouped into schools (the Impressionists, to take an example) would be regarded as being among the minor artists. Over and above the torments and passions of his characters, Bergman gives us a glimpse of a higher world. There is, in every icy glance of Liv Ulmann or in every monologue by Erland Josephson, a question as to the meaning of life, asked without ever being spoken. *Interiors* does not go beyond the wounds and reproaches that the characters inflict on each other. Here the transcendental inspiration is lacking. This gathering of the tormented rich is not overshadowed by ultimate questions, but rather by the connection of cause and effect between the different characters and the different neuroses. The psychoanalyst's couch replaces the mystical impulse. *Interiors* is a good dramatic film but it

is not a masterpiece, because Allen is not Bergman. But it is an extremely well written film and it is directed with skill and a sense of measure (even if the slightly melodramatic scene of Eve's suicide is a little embarrassing). The psychology of the characters is probed much more deeply than is usual in American cinema. Finally, its undeniable success at the box-office (which was considerable, if not vast) proves that it paints an easily recognisable picture of certain realities of its time.

As it is a dramatic and psychological film, it ought to be useful to analyse the characters of its protagonists. But this is not really necessary as

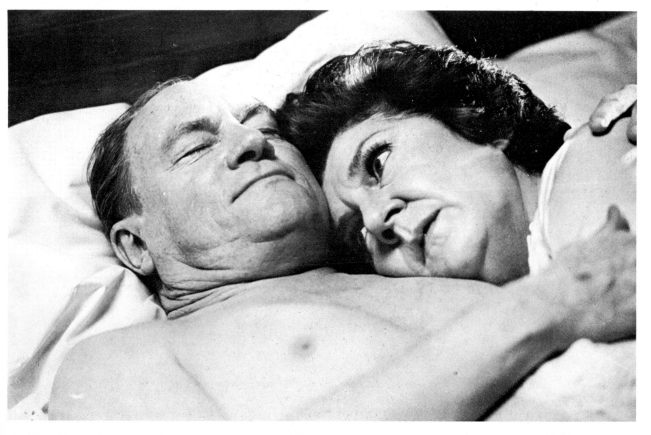

(Opposite) Eve.
(Left) Flyn (Kristin Griffith), in a shot which was cut in the final editing of the film.
(Below) Pearl.

they already analyse themselves very thoroughly. These men and women talk continually, they look deep into themselves and show an astonishing capacity for introspection. They are beings who know themselves and know those who are close to them. But this does not stop them from tearing each other to pieces with their beautiful, gleaming teeth. And they cannot be accused of acting out of spite nor an excess of love. So why then? Perhaps out of a sense of alienation. The notion of 'interiors' explains things very well. 'Would you mind closing the window? The street noises are just unnerving', says Eve on her first appearance. And throughout the rest of the film the noise of traffic is not heard. There are always lovely houses, large windows, a peaceful world inhabited by people who live as if they were in an aquarium. The only possible reaction to such an isolation is creativity, or else a radical alternative: to choose to be the vital, sensual Pearl rather than Eve. Pearl is far from being a paragon, but she is in complete contrast to Eve, and constitutes a sheet-anchor for a practical man like Arthur. His daughters, and their companions, on the other hand, are too effete and dedicated to their books to change their lifestyles. They have opted for creativity, which can offer

them not only success but also protection. Each to his own interior. Those who have succeeded in becoming established, like Renata, are contented, although no less in need of a psychoanalyst. The others are dissatisfied. The isolation of the characters leads also to a mutual incomprehension. In fact, there are hardly any real exchanges between the characters. And the film, or rather the dramatic action, suffers for this. There is a leaden sense of predestination which is almost Chekhovian and somewhat forced (someone rebaptised this film *The Three Sisters in New York*, partly as a joke and partly in criticism). The immobility produced by the counter-balancing tensions prevents us from being able to identify the pivot, the main protagonist in the film. The direction allows each actor to play an equal part, and it really is not possible to maintain that the real central character is the whole milieu, the family, or the group. To animate the film and make it expressive, Allen has had to call upon all the resources of the cinematic language. The set designs and the costumes were carried out, respectively, by Mel Bourne and Joel Schumacher, and their work here assumes a great importance. They create a perfect harmony of beige, ochre and grey, only interrupted by the loud clothes of the 'outsider',

The three sisters, Renata, Flyn and Joey, at the window overlooking the ocean, after the death of Eve.

Pearl. The actors are all excellent. Especially Geraldine Page (Eve), who plays with intelligence and subtlety the part of a character it would be easy to dislike. With consummate skill, Maureen Stapleton (Pearl) avoids the charge of slipping into caricature. Mary Beth Hurt, a newcomer, interprets the role of Joey, who is the most rich and alive character, probably the one with which the author most identifies himself. As for Diane Keaton, she is excellent in the dramatic register, although a certain mannerism does show through her performance at times. The camera often reveals cold and empty places, through which the characters wander onto the scene and off again. Even during the most difficult moments (like the monologue-confessions done in close-up with the actor looking directly at the audience), the actors always convey an impression of participation, once again giving witness to Allen's ability to involve his actors emotionally in the subject. The directing is highly stylised, spartan, to the point of renouncing any help from a soundtrack, with the exception of a few pieces of background music. This demonstration of the highest professionalism is almost excessive in its determination to have everything convey a 'meaning'. It smacks too much of the perfectionist, too involved and intense to allow anything superfluous to appear, a moment of relaxation or even a smile. As has already been said, a lack of humour is no more natural than its profusion. Nor can we hide the fact that this all-encompassing need to 'signify' sometimes leads to the mechanical use of worn out symbols which appear with the regularity of clockwork (the sea, the windows which divide the faces from reality).

Interiors marks an important moment in Woody Allen's creative output, both because, as we have already said, it shows the moral strength of a director who is firm in his decision to follow his own path rather than that of easy success, and because it shows that he has overcome his inferiority complexes: the complex of the comedian who 'sits at the childrens' table'; the complex of the filmmaker who is a little unsure of himself and has to protect himself with laughter; the complex of the Jew who feels dominated by WASPS, (remember the meal at the house of Annie's parents in *Annie Hall*). This time, Woody Allen succeeds in depicting, with a great deal of human interest, the tastes, the mentality and the sufferings of a wealthy American family. Everything is ready for the great fresco that will be *Manhattan*.

Manhattan

Images in black and white. Views of various streets in New York. 'Chapter one. He adored New York City. He idolised it all out of proportion . . .' The off screen voice of Woody Allen continues to try out a variety of beginnings for 'Chapter one', until he decides: 'New York was his town. And it always would be'. At this point George Gershwin's Rhapsody In Blue is heard and its crescendo mingles with the explosions of the 4th of July fireworks at night in Central Park. At a table in a restaurant we meet four of the main characters of the film: Isaac (Ike) Davis, forty year old television writer (Woody Allen), his seventeen year old girl-friend Tracey (Mariel Hemingway), his friend Yale, a university lecturer in literature (Michael Murphy), and Yale's wife Emily (Anne Byrne). They talk in fits and starts, and when they go out, Yale, walking side by side with Ike, cannot refrain from confiding his problem of the moment: although he is happily married, he is now infatuated with another woman, a beautiful journalist, a neurotic individual. . . . Ike meets her almost by accident several evenings later, at an exhibition to which he has gone with Yale. Her name is Mary (Diane Keaton) and she makes the worst possible first impression on him: snobbish, cold, intellectual, she even ends up by spotting a slit of 'over-rated' celebrities (amongst whom she includes Mahler, Jung, Fitzgerald and Boll) and in which she even names Ike's idol, Ingmar Bergman. In reality, Mary is hypersensitive, vulnerable, full of doubts, and her supercilious demeanour is only a façade, a protective shield. When Ike meets her again, this time alone, in another elegant setting, they end up by spending the whole night together, chatting and exchanging confidences.

The second meeting between Ike (Woody Allen) and
Mary (Diane Keaton), in the absence of Yale, at the
Museum of Modern Art.

*Dawn finds them side by side on a
bench overlooking the 59th Street
Bridge. But for the time being, Ike's
private life is a million miles from
Mary. Instead, he has an ambivalent
relationship with Tracey, a high-
school girl who almost thrusts her
love on him with innocent determination and who at times seems to him
too young as well as too demanding.
They live moments of great tenderness
together, but Ike obstinately continues
to put up barriers to protect himself
from the young girl's straightforward,
healthy sentiments. When an opportunity arises for her to go and study at
the Royal Academy of Dramatic Art
in London he encourages her in every
way that he can to take advantage of
it.*

*Ike has another personal problem:
Jill, his second ex-wife (Meryl Streep),
is currently involved in the draughting
of a retrospective critical book on
their marriage. Ike is worried by the
possibility that the 'disgusting little
moments' of his private life will be
exposed to the public in the windows
of bookshops, and he has a number
of arguments with her on this issue
without success. To make things
between them more difficult, there is
also their son to consider (in the care
of his mother) and the fact that Jill is
living with the woman for whom she
left her husband in the first place. One
fine day, Ike Davis comes to the conclusion that the television show for
which he writes the scripts has finally
gone beyond the limits of stupidity. In
an act of courage, he gives up everything and decides to write a book. It
will be necessary for him to economise
for a while, by moving to an apartment that costs less and by giving less
money to his father. ('He's not gonna
be able to get as good a seat in the
synagogue . . . he's gonna be in the*

133

The couples game.
(Left) Mary and Ike.
(Left, below) Ike and his second ex-wife Jill (Meryl Streep).
(Below) Yale (Michael Murphy) and his wife Emily (Anne Byrne).

back away from God.') In the meanwhile, the love between Mary and Yale encounters problems. Yale is being torn apart, between his wife and his mistress. Moreover, he has very little time to devote to Mary: and she is not the sort of person to tolerate being ignored. One Sunday, when her solitude weighs too heavily on her, and Yale is at dinner at his wife's parents' house, she telephones to ask Ike to go for a walk. They are caught in a storm and go into the planetarium for shelter. There, the softened lights and the models of the celestial bodies encourage the two neurotics to confide in each other again and an almost palpable communion is established between them. Thus it is more than natural that, when Yale, after the umpteenth argument with Mary, declares that their relationship is over, Mary should turn to his friend Ike for comfort. More than natural, also, that Yale himself should urge Ike to court Mary and that, in the end, Ike decides that a solution of this type would be in everyone's best interests. No sooner said than done: that which, deep down, is little more than mutual understanding, turns into living together and the person who loses most is Tracey, who is dismissed gently but without too much consideration on the very same day that she triumphantly brings a gift (a mouth organ) for the man of her dreams.

As could have been foreseen, the 'solution' resolves nothing. Mary really is 'trouble', as she says herself. She cannot succeed in getting Yale out of her mind. After having a surprise encounter with the first husband of his mistress, a short bald man ('a genius . . . an oversexed brilliant kind of animal', according to Mary), Ike has to endure the much worse shock of seeing her return to the arms of

Yale. Since, as we know, it never rains but it pours, the book written by his ex-wife Jill is published in the meantime, and Ike cuts a pitiful figure in it.

Yale and Mary, for now, live together, Ike is limited to some incoherent discussions with Yale (in a university classroom where a skeleton leans over to watch them!) and Emily, Yale's abandoned wife, accepts this new state of affairs with weary melancholy. Time passes. One day, stretched out on his couch, Ike begins to list 'Why is life worth living? . . . . There are certain things, I guess, that make it worthwhile.' They are, in order: Groucho Marx, the baseball player Willie Mays; the second movement of the Jupiter symphony; Louis Armstrong playing Potato-head Blues, Swedish films; Flaubert's A Sentimental Education; Marlon Brando; Frank Sinatra; Cezanne's still lifes; crabs from Sam Wo's restaurant and Tracey's face. Having completed his list, it is the last that seems the most important thing of all. Ike gets up from the sofa, potters about, opens a few drawers, until he finds the mouth organ, tries to telephone, and finally rushes out. He arrives at Tracey's house just at the moment when she is loading her bags for London. The young woman has never stopped loving him, but it is impossible for her to cancel her trip. She will be back in six month's time. Ike is afraid of the men she will meet in London, and he also fears that her innocence may be corrupted. Once again, we hear Rhapsody In Blue in the background. Tracey comforts our hero, saying: 'You have to have a little faith in people'. The music continues and the film ends in the same way it began, with views of Manhattan.

Manhattan's charm lies in the fact that it is a gamble which succeeds against all logic; unimportant events are narrated, selfish people are described, a rich and exclusive ambience is portrayed, both tenderness and romance are presented, and, despite all this, the film succeeds in being both credible and lyrical. In this film, Allen permits himself scenes and lines which would have caused the more sentimental script writers of the Thirties and Forties to wince. He risks showing Ike and Mary on a bench under the bridge at dawn, as in the most mawkish and sentimental postcard. He makes Ike say, when, for once, he lets himself go with Tracey: 'You're God's answer to Job. He would've pointed to you and said "I do a lot of terrible things, but I can also make one of these".'

Manhattan is a delicate balance made up of all its component parts: direction, photography, acting, music, pacing, each one of which harmonises

Between an ice-cream and a mouth-organ, Ike breaks off his relationship with Tracy (Mariel Hemingway). Mary has now stepped into his life.

Mary and Ike against the background of the 59th Street Bridge.

with the others to create a sense of living reality. In a minefield like that of taste and feelings, the public responded with unforeseen and surprising unanimity. At the end of the violent and bitter (even in terms of the cinema) Seventies, this entirely unfashionable comedy met with nothing but praise for its mellow tints.

In Manhattan, more than in any other of his films, Woody Allen reveals himself. The devotee of the cinema here raises his intellectual mask and presents us with an openly sentimental comedy. The critics, often more responsive to intelligence than emotion (which is too elusive and subjective), could have demolished this film. They did not even try. Hostile comments were so extremely rare that at one point the editor himself of a publication concerned felt it his duty to take up his pen in defence of the film. The writer Larry McMurtry accused Allen of creating for the screen a universe centred on Manhattan that was incomprehensible to anyone who did not have direct and prolonged personal experience of New York (*American Film*, September 1979). In the same issue, the editor Hollis Alpert felt obliged to write that the critics normally see hundreds of films each year and they end up despairing of ever coming across something that is 'infused with intelligence, wit, feeling, human understanding, with characters that seem real, genuine, in a film that has something to "say"'. *Manhattan*, he concluded, had arrived like blessed rain in a season of drought.

Manhattan, like all successful works, has a solid façade but many facets. To read all the different opinions expressed about the film is a salutary lesson in pluralism. To several reviewers the characters were 'absol-

(Below) Mariel Hemingway.
(Right) The Mary-Yale-Ike triangle. In the end, Ike is the one excluded.

utely not credible', whilst others underlined the realism with which the characters of *Manhattan* are portrayed. Some maintained that Allen's portrayal was 'ferociously ironic', others felt it intense and involving. There were those who saw the final scene as a message of hope ('You have to have a little faith in people'), and there were those who saw it as an epitaph for all feelings of love. To say nothing of those who judged immoral the criss-crossing between the couples and those who, on the contrary, praised the morality of the behaviour portrayed and the purity of the director's intent. The characters have a substance and a consistency of their own: Ike, Mary and Tracey share the limelight equally. As was the case with *Interiors*, the quality of the dialogue is of the highest order. Each character has their own way of talking, according to their temperament. Mary expresses herself in the most perfect literary jargon. Tracey employs the few, simple, direct phrases appropriate to an adolescent who has not yet realised (or accepted) that things and people are much more complex than they seem in the experience of a seventeen year old. The wisecracks sparkle all through the film, quick-fire, elegant, irresistible, so typical of all of Allen's work: they make the audience laugh, they give a specific character to Ike, and on several occasions they invest Mariel Hemingway with a bit of Woody Allen himself ('Rita Hayworth . . . Do you think I'm unaware of any event pre-Paul McCartney or something?').

The comedy in *Manhattan* is subtle, and it is one of the components in the fragile balance that makes the film so elegant. The scene which is perhaps the most comic of all is stressed so little that it has the effect of a delayed

A romantic outing on the lake in
Central Park. He languidly drops his
hand into the water and pulls it out
covered in filth.

action joke: it is the discussion
between Ike and Yale at the university, when one accuses the other of
having stolen his woman, and the
argument moves imperceptibly to a
moralistic diatribe on the meaning of
life and the way we should behave.
Woody Allen has not learned this
lesson in refinement from the films of
his comic predecessors, neither from
the brilliant comedies of the Thirties
and Forties (even if sometimes it
would not seem out of place to think
of Lubitsch), nor even from the American theatre. As Andrew Sarris
observes, 'He had to find European
models of bourgeois drama to replace
the American action archetypes.' In
particular, one thinks of Chekhov (if
one can be permitted to cite the
greats), who has come to mind before
when considering *Annie Hall* and
Interiors.

In his portrayal of Ike Davis, Allen
gives proof of his maturity as an actor
and an unexpected wealth of express-
iveness. To be honest, he still cannot
be compared to a Robert de Niro or a
Dustin Hoffman, to mention but two
outstanding actors of his generation,
and of equivalent exposure. But he
plays his part well enough, even in his
scenes as a 'lover', which could have
been a little unconvincing because of
his rather unorthodox physical
appearance. If the parts of Yale and
Emily do not give Michael Murphy
and Anne Byrne the chance to shine to
any great extent, then, on the other
hand, the portrait by Diane Keaton of
a capricious and spoilt intellectual is
both rich and varied. We cannot
truthfully speak of the creation of a
role, since the actress repeats a
number of the aspects of her acting
repertoire that had won her an Oscar
award already, but she is a marvellous
incarnation of the character. More-

over, the character is not a pleasant one, although full of charm. Exasperatingly egocentric, amoral, neurotic and agonising, Mary is a convincing centre of attraction for two men as different as Ike and Yale, and is ready to respond to both. The only truly original character in the film is Tracey, remarkably interpreted by the virtually inexperienced Mariel Hemingway. Tracey is the focal point for most of the gentleness contained in the film, and the actress confers on her role a captivating mixture of shrewdness, sensuality and naivety. When she is with Ike she is not in the least affected. She does not flirt either. She possesses an extraordinary maturity, ridiculous almost in its fullness, but a maturity greater than that possessed by any of the other protagonists in the film, even though theoretically they are adult. She embodies the message that Woody Allen wishes to convey at the end: a new trust in human beings, symbolised in this instance by a young woman who is full of integrity, and a new confidence in certain types of behaviour, represented here by a way of living which needs neither wisecracks (Ike), nor vague intentions to write books (Yale, perpetually in the throes of composing an interminable biography of O'Neill), to escape from its own contradictions.

But there are two other important 'characters' as well. First and foremost, New York, caressed by the extraordinary camerawork in unfashionable black and white by Gordon Willis. A New York which lives and breathes in the background, but which is omnipresent, with its famous places, like the Museum of Modern Art, Central Park, Elaine's Restaurant, the Russian Tearoom. Far from being simply the background, New York, so to speak, enfolds the characters in the

Two moments in the Mary-Ike story: a visit to the Museum of Modern Art and the shower of rain that surprises them during a walk.

course of their journeys through the city. Just as *Annie Hall* was a hymn to a woman, so *Manhattan* is Allen's love letter to his own city, New York. As it is seen through Woody Allen's eyes; through the prism of affection and not with the coldness of actuality; as if through the black and white of the films of his childhood and adolescence, and through the music of George Gershwin. Until now, only one other American film-maker has shown such an involvement with this metropolis, Peter Bogdanovich (*They All Laughed*), another New Yorker.

The other character who is omni-present in the film, although scarcely mentioned, is George Gershwin. New Yorker, Jewish, popular song writer who successfully became a 'serious' composer, a man of the theatre and the cinema, Gershwin appears to fascinate the Woody Allen he resembles so much. The soundtrack of the film is made up of music which is his and only his, beginning with *Rhapsody In Blue*. Gershwin illustrates the depths of nostalgia in Ike Davis, a man who is unknowingly but manifestly in search of an identity,

Mary has gone back to Yale. Lying on his couch, Ike lists the things for which life is worth living: Groucho Marx, the baseball player Willie Mays, the second movement of the *Jupiter symphony*, Louis Armstrong. . . .

even a simply historical one. Allen's direction in *Manhattan* is mature. It is flexible, apparently free of strain and tension, a well-balanced compound of many elements. This time the respects paid to the history of the cinema are few and little more than casual (Renoir, Bergman and W.C. Fields are cited in the dialogues, and *Chushingura* by Inagaki and *The Land* by Dovzenko are featured in a cinema poster in an insignificant frame). Apart from the odd photographic indulgence (above all in the scene in the planetarium) the director has kept well clear of formalism. For once Woody Allen is 'classic'.

Stardust Memories

The hero is seated in the carriage of a
train standing in a railway station. His
surroundings are squalid and illumi-
nated by a harsh light. His fellow pas-
sengers appear to be in a daze, and are
hellishly ugly. On the platform
opposite there is another train, full of
happy and beautiful people. They are
having a great time. A blonde girl
looks across at the hero and blows
him a kiss, with a movement which
brings to mind Marilyn Monroe. The
man decides to change trains in order
to join her, but while he is trying
desperately to open the doors or the
windows the train starts up and moves
off, carrying its cargo of hopelessness
and solitude. At the end, both groups
of travellers descend from their trains
at a rubbish dump by the sea, where
an enormous flock of seagulls has
gathered. This is a non sequitur for
us in the film but it makes sense and
surprises us. We discover that we have
been watching the ending of a film
that the director Sandy Bates (Woody
Allen) is showing to his producers.
The 'real' film begins here. The reaction of the producers to this preview is
negative: they are of the opinion that
success has changed Sandy from a
superb comedian into a pretentious,
self-absorbed pseudo-artist, and that
the film is bound to have poor takings,
especially in the provinces. After
the screening of his film and the
subsequent discussion, one dreary
event after another overtakes Sandy.
A traffic jam delays his chauffeur
driven Rolls-Royce; from the telephone in the car he learns that his
tennis lesson has been cancelled, then
his lunch with a famous journalist is
confirmed, as is his appointment with
his analyst. Inside his own home,
where a number of his collaborators
have come to harass him, he receives
the final blow: he has been invited for

Sandy Bates (Woody Allen), a successful comedy film-maker, looking for new modes of expression. (Below) His press agent (Renée Lippin).

the weekend to the Hotel Stardust, at a beach resort, where a well-known critic of the cinema has organised a retrospective of his films. It is not possible for him to refuse.

Another delicious non sequitur: memories come flooding back to him. He sees Dorrie (Charlotte Rampling) again, the only woman he has truly loved. Neurotic (we will discover later that she has ended up in a psychiatric clinic after the breakup of her relationship with Sandy), incestuous, troubled she is also tender and intelligent; 'two days a month she was the most exciting woman in the world, but the rest of the time she was a basket case'. From this point onwards the three levels of the story (the real film itself, the memories and the scenes from the making of the film) intersect and intermingle, at times further complicated by sequences from Sandy's so-called retrospective. At the Hotel Stardust very little of any substance takes place: Sandy's fans continually harass him with questions of the most depressing banality; a certain Daisy (Jessica Harper) arouses in him a much more than fraternal interest; Isobel, his current flame (Marie-Christine Barrault), leaves her husband and comes to keep him company, complete with all her attendant baggage and offspring. And Sandy is always at the centre of it all, pensive, blasé and absorbed in

149

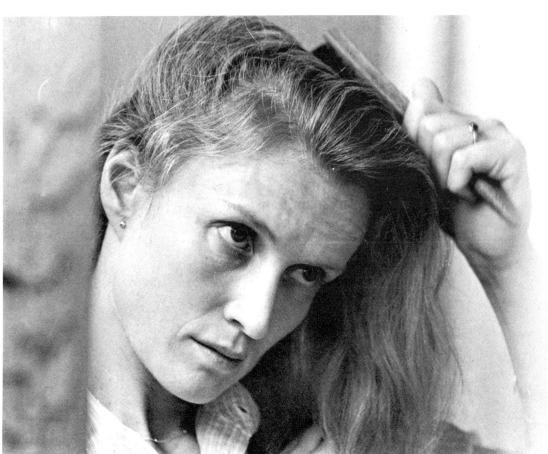

Sandy Bates' three women.
(Left) Daisy (Jessica Harper), the violinist who arouses
his interest at the hotel.
(Left, below) Isobel (Marie-Christine Barrault), his
current flame.
(Below) Dorrie (Charlotte Rampling), the only one he
truly loves.

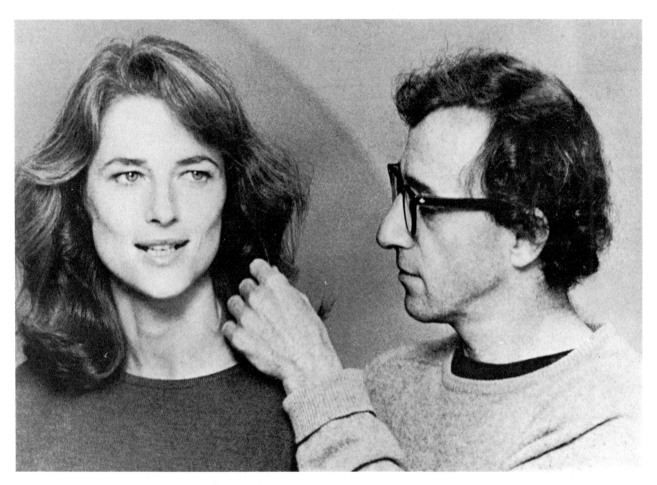

himself. Eventually, out in the countryside, he undergoes a hallucinatory experience, during which he meets up with some aliens, who tell him quite bluntly to stop taking himself so seriously and go back to making comedy films. Then one of his most fervent fans kills him. But this is a fantasy as well: so then we see Sandy passionately kissing Isobel, dispelling all doubts as to his attachment to her. But even this is not the true finale. In the real finale, all the characters solemnly leave the Stardust Hotel projection room in a sort of end of Show Parade, Sandy goes back alone, to get his glasses, and stare at the empty screen and the empty chairs.

Sandy's arrival in a Rolls-Royce, at the Hotel Stardust, where a retrospective of his films is taking place.

All the critics have noticed the close relationship between *Stardust Memories* and *8 1/2* by Federico Fellini; the decision to film in black and white, the overlapping of the story levels, a great number of small and large stylistic devices, and even the idea of the make-believe death of the hero in the final scenes. On the other hand, the comings and goings of the characters on the screen, which is often flat and empty, as well as certain passages from the scenes most filled with anguish, like the one in the rest-home where Dorrie mumbles her sick monologue into the camera, are taken from the repertoire of Ingmar Bergman.

If we pursued the dissection, we would find numerous other examples, from both these directors, and also from other less well-known filmmakers (like, for example, André Delvaux, the Belgian director of *One Evening A Train*). It is amazing that, after the limpid, mature masterpiece that is *Manhattan*, Allen should feel the need to draw on elements from his cinematographic culture as a means of expressing himself. But the problem with *Stardust Memories* is not so much its dependency on other models as its lack of real impulse. It conveys an impression of immobility, no spark of life could ever bring to life the juxtaposed fragments of which it is made up.

8 1/2 told of the contradictory, disorderly, Dionysian aspects of creation. The problem afflicting Sandy is much more prosaic than the one the Marcello of Fellini suffered from. He does not doubt for one moment his own ability to create. It is simply that he gets exasperated when he is told that his creative ability was greater when he was a comedian. Marcello's memories of his childhood were alive with the overflowing vitality of the countryside of Romagna; but in the memories of Sandy Bates there is neither love, nor hate, nor nostalgia. The gaunt Dorrie ends up by seeming more ill-favoured than the fleshy Saraghina, in the scene where she tenses the muscles of her waif-like body in an effort to open a bottle. As for Sandy, with his contempt for his admirers, his complex about being a victim of women, his moaning about producers, his whimsical comparisons between himself and God and his questioning of the aliens about his mission as an artist, all this has the irremediable effect of causing the audience to keep their distance from him. He is not a sympathetic character. He is a winner, an openly successful man (the first one in the gallery of all Woody Allen's characters), but despite his aura of obvious success, he remains always cold and aloof. He has no real communication with anyone, neither the other characters nor the public. Woody Allen's problem in *Stardust Memories* is above all an excess of zeal. The autobiographic element is present this time as well, but here he does not limit himself to translating it into images on the screen, he makes an exposition of it. It is not possible to count all the judgements and criticisms which are expressed about the protagonist, through the mouths of both the main characters and the minor ones in the background. 'What did you think the significance of the Rolls-Royce was?' asks a petulant female spectator of her friend. 'I think that it represents his car,' is the reply. In real life, Woody Allen actually does have a Rolls-Royce. The audience then does not even have to interpret the film. This means that it remains completely alien. The overall effect is, as always, seasoned with one-liners, but these

At the Hotel Stardust, Sandy's bothersome fans give him no peace, overwhelming him with banal and exasperating questions. Among them, only Daisy stands out from the crowd with her indifference.

tend to fall flat in a context totally
devoid of humour. Then Woody
Allen, as if to put the finishing touch
to a plot that has no *élan*, commits the
cardinal error. He searches around for
the 'beautiful' shot, the unusual angle,
the 'different' approach that will hold
the attention of the weary audience.
Niceties of photography and compo-
sition abound, but for all that there
is a sensation which has more of the
artisan about it than the artist.

So, can we say nothing but bad
things about *Stardust Memories*? No
– in spite of all, the film contains some
memorable sequences. By an irony of
fate, among these are the comedy
piece at his imaginary retrospective;
one of them at least (the flight of the
star's Aggressivity, personified by a
sort of huge gorilla) has the zany
inspiration of his early slapstick
works. Otherwise, the development of
the character of Daisy is well judged,
built up in a succession of little
touches. The evocative use of settings
reminds us of the 'throwaway' of
Allen's humorous period, his utilis-
ation of both the first and the second
shot. When Dorrie recalls the slightly

155

During the retrospective Sandy's current lover, Isobel, arrives to complicate the situation, bringing, along with her baggage, her children by her first husband.

wanton games of her adolescence with her father, the huge blow-up which decorates the wall is a reproduction of a newspaper cutting on the subject of incest. And when Sandy attempts to escape from his overbearing collaborators, talking to them about the suffering in the world, there is another giant blow-up on the wall, showing a Vietcong being threatened by a soldier with a pistol. Finally, and this really is the best moment of the film, one cannot forget the long lingering shot of Dorrie as she flicks through a news-

Even his daily life is a series of mishaps for Sandy. Here he argues with the cook who persists in trying to make him eat rabbit.

paper, looking at Sandy in a seductive way, while in the background Louis 'Satchmo' Armstrong sings *Stardust*. For a moment it is like being transported back to *Manhattan*, and one feels such regret that Allen did not maintain this personal and original impetus of his: describing human relationships with the greatest delicacy. So, at the end, we are left with the reiteration of Ike Davis' list; two good reasons for being alive, Louis Armstrong and a woman's face.

157

A Midsummer Night's Sex Comedy

New England at the dawn of the century. Leopold (José Ferrer) is an elderly and pompous university professor, immensely learned in many branches of knowledge. Having decided to abandon his celibate status, he is preparing to marry Ariel (Mia Farrow), an ex-free thinker who has left behind the sexual excesses of her recent past because she is obsessed by the fear of growing prematurely old. The two of them are getting ready to spend their last weekend together as fiancés in the country house of his cousin Adrian (Mary Steenburgen). Adrian is married to Andrew (Woody Allen) who has a job on Wall Street, an obsession for eccentric inventions, and a good friend called Maxwell (Tony Roberts), who is a doctor and a lady-killer. Maxwell, too, is invited for the weekend and he brings Dulcy (Julie Hagerty), a nurse from the hospital where he works, whom he has seduced for the occasion. And so we have these six characters united in the country house, in midsummer, when the senses heat up and the magic of the forest is everywhere. There is no shortage of catalysts. The owners of the house are no longer sexually compatible, because Adrian has become cold and tense; the bride and groom to be are ill-matched for reasons both of age and character; and between Maxwell, a Casanova in trousers and Dulcy, a Casanova in a skirt, there is almost no dialogue.

The walks in the woods and the meaningful looks begin to get things brewing. In the past, Andrew and Ariel had had an innocent flirtation with each other. So innocent that it has left them both wanting to satisfy their curiosity. Now, however, Maxwell too desires Ariel. Leopold watches over his wife-to-be with one eye, but with the other he looks with longing at Dulcy. The intrigues multiply, the lovers look for and lose each other, while the improbable inventions of Andrew complicate (or perhaps favour) things. There is even a Parapsychological sphere, a sort of magic ball which allows communication with the spirits and opens the door to the world of magic and the afterlife. Amidst these spells and desires, night falls, after a performance by Leopold as a lyric singer. Each of them meets their own fate. Leopold goes to bed with Dulcy and dies from ecstasy; Ariel, after having dreamt of taking up her relationship with Andrew again, happily accepts the attentions of Maxwell, very much in love, for the first time in his life! Adrian confesses a small betrayal (she too had succumbed to the charms of the handsome doctor), rediscovers her sexual ardour and puts her marriage with Andrew back on the rails.

The warm and golden tones of Gordon Willis' photography lend enchantment to this insubstantial story, as does the background music by Mendelssohn, conducted by Bernstein, Stefanov, and Ormandy. The magic, the protestations of love and the exchanges between lovers, and the sylvan setting, are all derived from Woody Allen's two great tutelary deities, Shakespeare and Bergman, from *A Midsummer Night's Dream*' and *Smiles On A Summer's Night*. We also recognise in passing the influence of the less august Walt Disney, particularly in the finale when glittering little spirits hover in the starry sky. . . .

As for the traditional Woody Allen,

Leopold (José Ferrer), an elderly university professor, is one of the guests of Adrian (Mary Steenburgen) for the midsummer weekend in her country house.

158

Adrian and (right) her guests.
(From the left) Maxwell (Tony Roberts), doctor and ladykiller, Leopold and his fiancée Ariel (Mia Farrow); Dulcy (Julie Hagerty), Maxwell's partner for the occasion.
(Right, below) Leopold with Dulcy, who will prove fatal for him.

it is mostly only traces that show through. For the first time, the character that he plays, Andrew, is just one of the group. He does share some traits with other Allen heroes (sexual frustration and the conflict between doing things and merely thinking about them), but he is basically integrated and easy-going, with a sound marriage that is temporarily in difficulties. If one stretched things, one could say that Andrew is an Ike Davis who has finished getting into scrapes after having married his Tracey. That the character played by Allen should

be so dull is probably not by chance. This 'sex comedy' is, in effect, the least Allen-like of all his films, the least designed as a mirror in which to reflect himself. For the first time in his career, he seems to have deliberately set out to 'manufacture' rather than 'create': to produce by choice a 'lesser' work, in which the stamp of his personality would be impressed only on the surface. In interviews, Allen has always affirmed his aversion to both summer and the countryside. If we do not bear in mind that the film is essentially an exercise in style, we could be

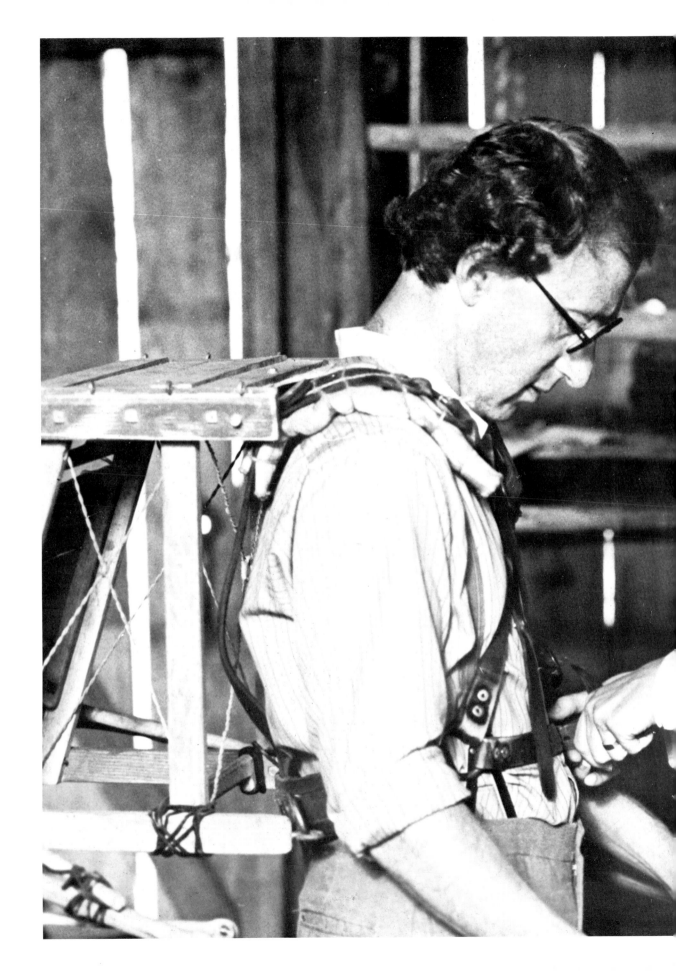

The owners of the house.
Adrian helps her husband Andrew
(Woody Allen) to prepare for the
testing of one of his eccentric
inventions.

taken aback by these images of arca-
dian love and luxuriant summer.

In reality, the film is very light, like
gauze, hazy. At times it is amiable and
playful, at times discreetly melan-
cholic, but in the end there is very little
substance. What is more, we are really
dealing with four films in one. There
is, primarily, the 'fairy-film', the fairy-
tale of nature populated by elves and
fairies and spells, of a golden summer,
and desires which trouble the body
and the spirit. There are, here, more
traces of Shakespeare than there might
at first seem, from *A Midsummer
Night's Dream* to *The Tempest* (one
of the characters is even called Ariel).
But the 'fairy-film' does not materi-
alise: it remains a suggestion, an allusion, a background. There is also the
comedy of manners. Woody Allen has
already proved that he excels in this
genre, and it offers us what is perhaps
the best scene in the film: when
confronted with an enigmatic projection by the parapsychological ball,
each one of the characters present
gives an interpretation which accords
with their own personal problems.

But the comedy of manners too, is
barely sketched in. Moreover, one
cannot even say that a light comedy
takes over. It is true that there are
encounters, assignations missed, assignations kept, changes of partner; but
the whole rhythm of the genre is
absent, all the refined play of the
misunderstandings.

Finally, comedy of the old Allen
type is found every so often, with all
the force of his originality: in particular in the nonsensical jokes that come
from first one, and then another of the
characters. This originality, however,
seems more to contrast with the film
as a whole than to harmonise with it.
Perhaps the different elements are by
their very nature irreconcilable, or

163

(Left) The Spiritualist experiment with the parapsychological sphere (from the left: Ariel, Andrew, Dulcy, Adrian and Leopold). The night falls amidst spells and magic, while the intrigues thicken and the lovers pursue and lose each other.
(Left, below) Dulcy.
(Below) Ariel.

perhaps Woody Allen's screenplay ('this' particular Woody Allen) is incapable of reconciling them. In any case, the audience leaves the cinema with a sense of satisfaction, for the positive aspects are undeniable, mixed with a sense of frustration, as if certain promises had not been kept. The real novelty in the film is the 'fairy' aspect: a real gamble, this, for an author so centred on the turmoil of existence and modern city life in particular. This is, moreover, a difficult stylistic choice, both because it presupposes rare qualities such as gaiety and lightness of touch, and because such qualities seem to be lacking in a director who had always diagnosed in himself, a 'dyseptic anhedonism'. And, in the face of all the evidence, the experiment does not appear very successful. The reason for this lies at the heart: this 'fairy-tale' suffers from a basic deficiency. It is not pagan. What magic there is in the film (the parapsychological sphere, the apparitions, and even the conversations on the subject) has more of the air of the occultism of a middle class drawing-room, than of the leafy forests of Oberon and Ariel. The paganism of the senses and of the midday hour (brought, for example, totally to life in Bo Widerberg's film *Elvira Madigan*), here gets drowned in aestheticism. The photography is too 'beautiful', the period settings are too 'pretty' and when the characters join with each other or part from each other, it is not a surrendering to the forces of Instinct and Desire, but simply a matter of yielding to a whim. We should praise the virtuosity of the costume designer, Santo Loquasto, who has been given ample opportunity to display his talents in this film. He has dressed the characters in fresh summery outfits, with straw

(Left) The picnics and the excursions into the woods favour exchanges between the couples.
(Left, below) Ariel, Leopolds's bride-to-be, dreams of taking up again an old flirtation with Andrew, but ends up by surrendering to the insistent courtship of Maxwell (below).

hats, and long loose gowns, always in tones of beige and ochre tints; and even the irresistible ankle-length bathing costumes are all taken from turn-of-the-century engravings. The actors perform with relaxed assurance, often in roles that are self-parodying; José Ferrer, who long ago won an Oscar, stands out on his return to the cinema after a long absence. Just as relaxing and sure is the directing of Woody Allen, a master of entrance and off-screen dialogues. Always very carefully controlled, the camera-work shows no apparent strain and discreetly records the sequence of events.

Zelig

Black and white images from a documentary film of the Thirties. It is a big parade in New York: somebody is being honoured, a hero. Who? Leonard Zelig. According to the writer, Susan Sontag, when she was interviewed about him, a man who was in his time as much of a celebrity as Lindbergh. Here, then, is the story of Zelig, narrated through the medium of 'archive' photographs and newsreels, together with a couple of extracts from a supposed biographical film produced by Warner in 1935, and comments from the people who knew him, and with analyses supplied by a number of contemporary intellectuals.

A humble New York worker, Leonard Zelig, disappears. He has left only two photographs of himself: in one he appears alongside the dramatist Eugene O'Neill, and in the other he is dressed like Canio, in the opera I Pagliacci. A short while later, in the Chinese quarter of the city, the police pick up an Asian male who resembles him greatly. He is sent to Manhattan Hospital where he begins to show the signs of his astonishing syndrome: he becomes almost 'identical' to the people with whom he is in contact, obese with the obese, black with the black, a doctor with doctors. On the radio and on newsreels all the hospital specialists spell out their own favourite diagnosis, no matter how far-fetched. But the only one to make any progress in fathoming Zelig's mind is a young doctor by the name of Eudora Fletcher, who breaks through by means of hypnosis. 'I want to be like other people because I want to please them,' is what, in substance, Zelig tells her when he is in one of his trances. And this is how Eudora explains the mystery: just like a chameleon, Zelig protects himself by assuming the aspects of the people around him.

The mass media, already on the alert, are enchanted by the idea of a human chameleon. They talk of nothing else. As we know, fame is money. Leonard's sister, Ruth, rushes to the hospital and takes her brother into her charge: after which, she exhibits him in circuses and theatrical arenas all over the world. He is all the rage and his fame spreads far and wide. One photograph shows Zelig between President Coolidge and the presidential candidate, Hoover; another immortalises him beside the most famous boxer in the world, Jack Dempsey. Songs are composed about him. Even Cole Porter would have written one if he could have found a word to rhyme with 'elig'. Success however, does not cure him of his loneliness. Doctor Fletcher has not forgotten about him and tries every legal means to have him entrusted to her care: but she is unsuccessful. The situation only changes when fate takes a hand. During a tour of Spain, his sister cum teacher cum manager gets into a quarrel with her jealous lover. During the night a blood-bath ensues, in the court of which both Ruth and her lover die, as well as the Spanish bullfighter who is the cause of the trouble. Unexpectedly, Zelig finds himself free again. And he disappears. In the meantime, public attention is distracted by other completely unconnected events. It is 1929, and the Wall Street Crash overwhelms the American nation. A diplomatic incident leads to the rediscovery of the strange little man, when he appears on the balcony in the Vatican alongside no less a person than the pope himself. Sent back to New York, he is readmitted to Manhattan Hospital, and luck is with him on this occasion. Eudora Fletcher will be responsible for treating him. The doctor installs

A photograph of Zelig (Woody Allen), the hero of the mass-media, standing between the President, Calvin Coolidge, and the presidential candidate, Herbert Hoover.

Zelig standing beside Eugene O'Neill. This is one of the two pictures of Zelig which remain after he disappears for the first time.

her patient in her own house in the country, and seeks to penetrate his neurotic defences. Using a little hypnosis and a little subterfuge, she succeeds in germinating the seeds of the autonomous personality which is hidden at the heart of our chameleon. A mutual feeling also develops between them, so that the revealing of their love goes hand-in-hand with Zelig's progressive recovery. The public is delighted: the female doctor has defeated the powers of evil, 'and, she's pretty, too!' The couple become celebrities and there are kind words and smiles from everybody. A triumphal marriage is in prospect. Then there is drama. Firstly, Lita Fox, an ex-music hall actress, makes the accusation that Zelig had married and then abandoned her. One by one, dozens of other cases of breach of trust and thoughtless acts of stupidity come to light, all committed by Zelig when he was out of his mind. With the same enthusiasm with which they had exulted him, the public now condemn him. He fights back and defends himself bravely in court. But the crises continue to come at him and he grows unstable and disappears again. This time his disappearance seems to be permanent. Eudora devotes herself entirely to searching for him. Then, one evening, in exhaustion she agrees to go to the cinema with her sister. They see Grand Hotel *and they also watch the accompanying newsreel. In a piece of film from Germany, in which Hitler and his entourage appear, there is a glimpse of a well-known face. Zelig a Nazi? Eudora chooses to believe her own eyes and sets out at once for Europe. She gets as far as Munich, and arrives there during a huge rally at which the Führer is present. Here, to her astonishment she finds Zelig, immediately*

Having become a celebrity, the human chameleon,
Leonard Zelig is immortalised alongside great people.
Here, he is with the heavyweight champion of the world,
Jack Dempsey.

behind the great leader, among his most faithful followers. In the midst of all the crowd, Eudora waves in an attempt to get Zelig's attention. He catches sight of her, his mind clears, and he waves back. There is a rumpus and Hitler is extremely offended. The couple escape to the airport. A clip from the German newsreel, UFA Tonwoche, shows the flight of the two Americans. Like a chameleon again, Zelig changes himself into a pilot and succeeds in scraping home, though in an unorthodox manner. He cannot hold the aeroplane properly on its course and they make the Atlantic crossing upside down. A record. It is the end of their tribulations. The Americans love records, and love stories with a happy ending. Once again, the whole world is on his side. The city of New York honours him (these are the triumphant scenes we witnessed at the beginning of the film). As soon as the legal actions are resolved, the marriage of Leonard and Eudora is celebrated; Zelig can now slip into happy anonymity and will be able to recover completely from his illness.

The psychiatrist Eudora Fletcher succeeds in discovering the hidden motive for Zelig's transformism: it is simply the result of his desire to be like other people in order to please them.

2

Take The Money And Run and, even more, the censored *The Politics Of Woody Allen* had already taken the form of a false biographical documentary, using archive film material as well as scenes specifically shot for the work. In the case of *Zelig*, the idea is more ambitious and absolutely new. The whole film is passed off as an assembly of authentic newsreels, in such a way that a completely fictitious story (and a totally implausible one at that) is presented as a testimony to an epoch. We should take our hats off to this remarkable technical achievement. Woody Allen and Mia Farrow fit into fifty year old frames with perfect naturalness, as, by means of truly expert trick photography, they hug Josephine Baker or James Cagney. And this is not all. The whole film is a pot-pourri of sequences put together as if they were made in that epoch, as well as archive film of the time, either in its original form or 'distorted'. The 'grain' of the film would deceive even the most experienced eye. The lighting is done in the style of the period, there are 'rain-type' streaks to give the effect of worn film and there are variations in the lighting between one scene and the next. The sound is metallic, with an echo like that on the early *Movie-*

tones. The words and the tone of the spoken comments seem to have come from the archives as well. The brand new songs written for the film by Dick Hyman (*Leonard The Lizard*, *Doin' The Chameleon*, *Chameleon Days*, *Reptile Eyes*, etc.) are totally in keeping with the musical style of Fats Waller and company. All this is the work of a highly talented counterfeiter, obsessively meticulous. But it is not simply a matter of technical virtuosity. In a certain sense we could say that Allen has had the creative brilliance to rebuild an entire world (that of the Twenties and Thirties) and record it on film. The tastes, the customs, the ways of thinking, are reproduced with precision and love, as if this American, born in 1935, had always been immersed in the atmosphere of the Twenties, Prohibition and the Jazz Age. A person with a chameleon character is therefore depicted by a chameleon film.

Who is Leonard Zelig? Above all, he is a man seeking to be part of society. His transformations amount to an initiation rite: he wishes to be acceptable. This rite, however, is not really efficacious. No matter how well the 'chameleon' merges with his background he is still 'different'. He suc-

ceeds in resembling something, but not in giving himself an identity. Nevertheless, Leonard Zelig, without realising it, does society a great service: he acts as a mirror to it and shows it all the facets of which it is composed. Thus his role becomes a precious and rare one, like that of the artist, the actor or the clown. The man who would like to be everybody, reveals himself to be unique and inimitable. In the same way, the film creates its impression with its imitative perfection. The great creators of 'copies' have often affirmed that the counterfeiting of a masterwork by an artist is a highly stimulating intellectual adventure: it is necessary to retrace all the stylistic and technical choices made by the master, and to relive his emotions and his intuitions. In 'copying' the Twenties and Thirties, in 'copying' an American adventure, *Zelig* permits us, on its different levels, to examine the characteristics of an epoch, of a country and a people.

Moreover, there are the metamorphoses of the director. The creative path of Woody Allen himself, through all its different phases, is thick with models and imitations. On each occasion that he set out to imitate something, he has ended up by rediscovering himself. Thus, one of the least obvious aspects of the film *Zelig* is that it is, without doubt, a self-portrait of the author. Having concluded, at least temporarily, his examination of isolated individuals (which he began with *Annie Hall*), with this film Allen returns to his studies of society. In the event, he himself has declared that the film does not deal with a character so much as the reactions which society makes to the stimulus which he represents. 'Otherwise', Allen concludes, 'this

Zelig under the effect of hypnosis. This is one of the methods used by Eudora Fletcher to reveal in him a genuinely autonomous personality.

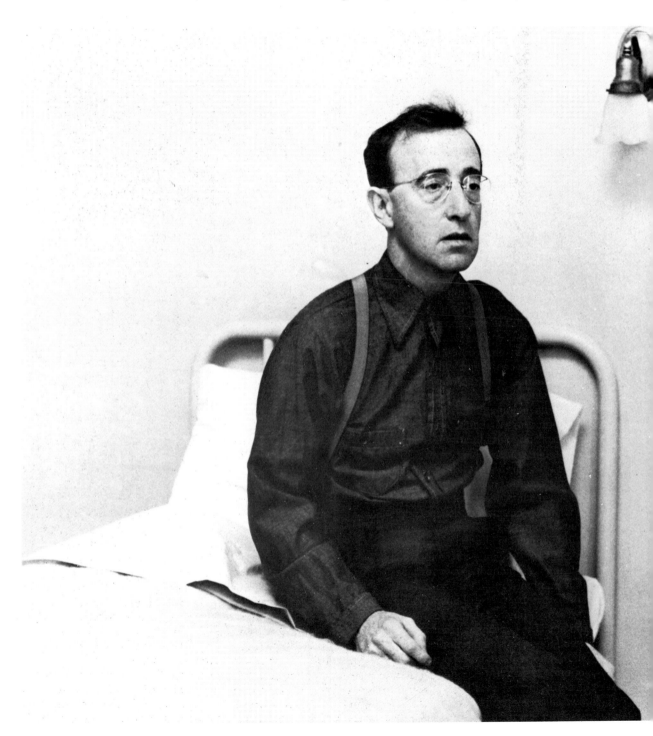

would be nothing more than the pathetic tale of a neurotic.' The film carries within itself an implicit message which the audience is invited to decipher. In many instances, in fact, the plot is set aside and the message is offered in explicit terms. At times, it is the hero himself who takes part ('I'm a democrat. I always have been'; 'One has to be oneself, otherwise one is like a robot or a chameleon'). In other instances, the keys to understanding are offered by the intellectuals interviewed in the film. Bruno Bettelheim, the psychoanalyst, maintains that Zelig is not so much a special case, but rather an example pushed to the extreme of something which is common: the conformist. The writer Saul Bellow is not at all surprised that Zelig, although Jewish, ends up amongst Hitler's Brown Shirts: like many people he is desperate to be part of the mob, 'and Fascism is the type of movement which can satisfy this need.' Irving Howe, a specialist in American Judaism, stresses that fundamentally Zelig embodies 'the immigrant Jew's need for integration in his new American homeland.' These are not the only possible points of view, naturally. But, in one way or another, Woody Allen proposes and underlines these. And he is not afraid anymore of expressing himself in the matter of sentiment. The most moving moments in this film (which is otherwise coolly intelligent) are those which show the blossoming of love between Leonard

177

(Left) Two of Zelig's metamorphoses; with the doctors, he is a doctor. He is French with the French (Left, below).
(Below) The triumphal return to New York after his incredible adventures in Nazi Germany and the upside-down flight across the Atlantic.

and Eudora. A smile, a gesture, a moment of embarrassment, and Mia Farrow becomes enchanting while Woody Allen is tender, awkward, affectionate. The importance of love is also clearly stated by the voice of another supposed witness, no less than Francis Scott Fitzgerald: 'Wanting people to like him, Zelig would change himself beyond recognition. However it was not the approval of the masses but the love of a woman that changed his life.'

Finally, it should not be forgotten that *Zelig* is also a comic film. The very idea of the chameleon-man is a great comic absurdity. The one-liners, the wisecracks, run through the screenplay like an electric current, sometimes perhaps uncontrolled, but sparkling and hilarious all the same. And, for sure, Leonard Zelis is very funny. Often, according to the best traditions, despite himself and unknown to himself. He is comical in his metamorphoses, in his movements, and in his relationships with the doctors, who, in trying to cure him, twist him out of shape, grind him up and make him submit to the most improbable tests. Even his name, which in Yiddish means 'blessed' is comical in a character who, paradoxically, is beset by so much misfortune. Even if laughter is no longer his principal aim, Allen shows here that he remains, both as an author and an actor, a humourist of the highest quality.

Broadway Danny Rose

It is an evening just like all the others at the Carnegie Delicatessen on Broadway (or more familiarly, the Carnegie Deli), a popular meeting place for show business people. A group of comedians have gathered together. They are Sandy Baron, Corbett Monica, Jackie Gayle, Morty Gunty, Will Jordan, Howard Storm and Jack Rollins, all playing themselves. They begin to gossip and tell each other stories. Their favourite topic of conversation, the one they find the funniest, is Broadway Danny Rose. Who is this character? He is a small time agent, always handling clients who are even bigger flops than he is, but who is unquenchable in his passion for show business and who looks after his protegés with a fierce, protective zeal. Danny Rose (Woody Allen) represents the most down and out artists you could imagine: there is a blind xylophonist, a one-legged tap dancer, a hypnotist who cannot guarantee to wake up the people he hypnotises. Danny Rose gives them all his full support. He pacifies the husband of a hypnotised woman by promising him that, if she does not wake up, he will take care of his meals himself, bringing him along to a restaurant; he offers at the 'old price' (i.e. 'anything you want to pay') the services of a woman who makes music out of wineglasses; he hands out advice and support, for example drawing the 'three S's' (Smile, Strong Star) to the attention of an elderly couple who specialise in making animal-shaped balloons. But the greatest of all Broadway Danny Rose's adventures is told by Sandy Baron, who insists that the others keep quiet and listen to him. It is the story of Lou Canova, and it is effectively the story of the film.

Lou Canova (Nick Apollo Forte) is

(Clockwise from the extreme left) Morty Gunty, Corbett Monica, Sandy Baron, Will Jordan, Jack Rollins, Howard Storm, Jackie Gayle (all playing themselves), laughing at the misadventures of Danny Rose in the Carnegie Delicatessen.

an overweight forty year old, whose only claim to fame is that he was a reasonably well-known child singer during the Fifties. He is not a bad guy, but, apart from a tendency to drink too much, his repertoire is poor to say the least, his talent is very limited, and he has an amateurish stage presence and an over-favourable opinion of himself! He still sings, but only in bars and taverns, and Danny Rose adores him. He fusses over him, encourages him, and consoles him when necessary. When 'nostalgia' comes back into fashion, this post-war relic comes back into favour, and gradually he begins to get better offers. And, at last, the chance of a lifetime presents itself: a television spectacular on the theme of 'nostalgia', to be staged at the Waldorf Astoria and presented by the famous Fifties comedian, Milton Berle. If all goes well, Lou will leap to nationwide fame, and Danny will finally have an important client. But Lou has another weakness: women. He has been through a number of divorces and re-marriages, but at this time he is madly in love with a certain Tina Vitale. Without her by his side, Lou will never be able to give a worthwhile performance on the evening at the Waldorf Astoria; but how can it be arranged? Being a married man he cannot parade her at his side. Danny will have to go and get the girl, and bring her to the show as if she was his girl-friend: acting as the decoy, the camouflage. Ever faithful to the teachings of a wise old uncle of his ('acceptance, indulgence, love') Danny Rose agrees. But Tina Vitale (Mia Farrow) is a lady to beware of. The ex-wife of a ganster who has passed on ('certain people shot him between the eyes' is her explanation for his demise), Tina sports a mane of bleached blonde hair and a large pair of dark glasses. She

Nicknamed 'Broadway' because of his passion for show business, Danny Rose (Woody Allen) is a minor theatrical agent always dealing with clients even more unsuccessful than himself.
(Right) One of these is Lou Canova (Nick Apollo Forte), a has-been Italian-American singer.

has a nasal Brooklyn accent, a permanent wad of chewing-gum in her mouth, and a fierce temper. Just before the brave Danny arrives to pick her up, she has a fight with Lou, decides to have no more to do with the singer and rushes out, leaving him to his fate. Typically, Danny does not give up, and within an hour he succeeds in tracking her down to a rendezvous for Italian Americans, filled with shady looking characters. The girl agrees finally to return to Manhattan with Danny and attend Lou's performance: except that meanwhile another complication has arisen. There are certain people who think that Danny is the gallant beau who sends a white rose each day to Tina (in reality, of course, it is Lou). Old flames are re-ignited, jealousy rears its head, and honour must be vindicated. The trip to the Waldorf Astoria turns into an odyssey of chases, capture and escapes. The couple reach their destination just in time, only to find that Lou Canova is drunk. Danny sobers him up and sends him onto the stage. And success arrives at long last. But watching the show also, there is an important agent, who has been asked to come beforehand by Tina. He decides to accept Lou Canova as one of his clients, to turn him into a star. It is the apotheosis of ingratitude. Lou tells Danny about the new arrangements, and Tina does not say a word, in spite of the fact that she knows the efforts

that the little man has made on Lou's behalf.

A year passes. Canova has moved to California and abandoned his New York flame. Without really knowing why, Tina is nervous and unhappy. Then finally, almost by chance, she remembers that odd character, Broadway Danny Rose, and decides to go and see him. In his modest apartment, Danny is celebrating Thanksgiving Day, along with the lamentable collection of clients who remain with him. They are making the most of a poor meal when the doorbell rings and Tina appears. She asks him to forgive her. Amazed and bitter, he refuses and sends her away. Then he has second thoughts and he rushes out to look for her, as a few snowflakes begin to fall. He finds her, and reconciled at last, together they make their way back to the house.

As is obvious, the plot is a very simple one, with few intellectual pretensions. A 'little' film of the kind Woody Allen loves to make, perhaps more 'little' than usual since it was conceived almost as a filler between two major intellectual efforts (*Zelig* and *The Purple Rose of Cairo*), and also as a vehicle for Mia Farrow, for the first time in her career playing an aggressive, vulgar role. But, since the film comes from the cameras of one of the greatest film-makers around today, it is worth looking into it at greater depth.

First of all, the characters. Danny Rose is perhaps Allen's best interpretation as an actor. This achievement was probably made easier by the fact that the part is so completely different to that of his usual alter-ego, the neurotic, complex ridden, Manhattanite intellectual. By keeping his distance from this role, Allen has also managed to go beyond it. Danny is a small, sweet mediocrity, not the caricature of a failure. He has a limited intellect, not the neurosis of a clumsy genius. He is not so much a Woody Allen character, as a character from Damon Runyon, the extraordinary chronicler of 'Guys and Dolls' from the early

decades of the century. And Danny does not wear the usual clothes which Allen chooses directly from his own personal wardrobe: he wears impossibly long jackets with impossibly dark spotted shirts. He is a character drawn from memory. During his debut years in the Fifties and in cabaret in the years which followed, Allen bumped into such sweet strange simpletons almost daily, incurably in love with show business, and, through their trade, busily trying to survive inside this love affair. By waving his arms about animatedly, by controlling his partiality for 'intelligent' jokes (only a couple of funny but out of place gags reveal the old 'Woody' under the disguise of Danny); and, above all, by the controlled emotion of his playing in the two final scenes with Tina in his little apartment, Allen really has on this occasion challenged Charlie Chaplin on his own ground.

The character of Tina Vitale is also very well portrayed by Mia Farrow. As we said earlier, this film was created in part as a homage from Allen to an excellent actress who had previously been limited, or limited herself, to playing the role of a young girl, fragile as a flower. The story goes

Danny with Tina Vitale (Mia Farrow), the woman with whom Lou is madly in love.

that one day in a restaurant, Mia saw a woman like Tina, with heavy make-up and brassy tinted hair. She pointed her out to Allen and expressed a desire to play a character like that on the screen.

The variations in the depth of her voice (normally like a teenager's), her coarse gestures and actions, add greatly to the characterisation of the Italian American, brusque and disagreeable, but loyal within the limitations of her own moral code, and sincere within the limits of her pride.

Finally, to round off the tributes to the actors it must also be said that the ex-fisherman, aspiring singer, Nick Apollo Forte, is an inspired choice for the role of Lou Canova. The voice and the songs of Forte are just as nearly acceptable as the character requires, and his self-centred, greedy, baby face tells us more about the character than we would get from lots of dialogue or dramatic scenes.

It is a film, therefore, about memories. It is narrated like a fairy-tale, or like a reminiscence, by the small-time actors who meet up regularly in a show business bar, talking always about the times they had in the good old days. With free-flowing elegance the film revolves around the Carnegie Deli, in an atmosphere of legendary recollection. Periodically, the action returns to the delicatessen to interrupt the direct narrative and allow the group of comedians listening to Sandy Baron's story to put in a word. At the Carnegie Deli, Danny catches up with Tina for their final reunion; it is in the Carnegie Deli that Danny takes refuge when he is betrayed by Lou. Like Chaplin before him, Allen plays a heartfelt homage to the limelight he knew in his youth.

Of course, the film is a comedy. As we have said, a few jokes escape the little agent, to float about in the rarefied air of the absurd and move the public to laughter. A whole series of situations are very funny; especially those concerning the Italian American community, filmed in all its excesses (people ripping up bank notes, fat babies stuffing themselves with ice-cream) with icy camera-work that might almost be directed by Federico Fellini.

Danny and Tina's escape is also very funny, first as they untie their bonds with a rhythmic swaying which is similar to an erotic ritual, and then as they dodge bullets in a warehouse full of carnival masks, (at this point it is worth explaining a diverting comic invention that is not always appreciated: the Donald Duck-like voice distortions in this scene are justified by the leakage of compressed helium for the containers punctured by the bullets. The increase in air pressure has the effect of distorting voices.)

To sum up, it is plain to see how fraught with difficulties the film *Broadway Danny Rose* really was. It mixes comedy and tenderness, fine sentiments and nostalgia, minor Broadway myths and sad clowns: and it does all this in these disenchanted modern times, when Chaplin has just been indicted as a false genius and classified as a fine example of bad taste. How could Allen win this contest? And if he has triumphed, it is because he has turned again to the *Manhattan* recipe: directing seriously, with great attention to detail, with a light touch and no formalistic ambitions (or very few formalistic ambitions); the use of black and white which lends itself so well to a dreamy realism, a mastery of cinematographic language which has few rivals in the whole world.

Finally, one must not ignore the ethical implications. Of course, Danny is funny when he lectures to Lou, because, having been married and divorced several times, Lou's had his head turned by this Tina Vitale from New Jersey. He is funny when he bursts out with 'But what kind of woman is she, if she knows you are married?' He is even funny when he preaches well-being and success to every down and out he comes across, even to Tina herself when she wants to furnish his apartment in the style of an African jungle. He is even funny when he holds up as examples some of his down and out relatives in support of certain rules of good behaviour. But, in the end, the film does not attempt to belittle Danny's choices, even though it underlines their uselessness in the practical life of a modern city. It is a fairy-tale, but a fairy-tale with its own internal morality and message. Tina, tough and pragmatic, a strong supporter of the theory 'grab what you can, and if you can rip someone off, rip him off before he does it to you', lives an unhappy life. She is filled with feelings of guilt towards the little man, because, thanks to her, he lost the client he had almost died for. In a simplified and somewhat sweetened version, this film is a development of the lines of thought that Allen had once expressed in an interview 'Life is like a concentration camp. There are some people who betray their best friends, and there are others who behave with incredible courage.'

The Purple Rose of Cairo

Right from the credits, the enchanting melody of Cheek To Cheek puts the audience into the mood for the film. These are the magical Thirties, when Hollywood was the collective all-American dream, just as the economic crisis was its nightmare. The film's central character is Cecilia (Mia Farrow). She is skinny, unkempt, poor, and not very pretty. She works as a waitress in a snack-bar; she has a bull-headed, demanding husband (Danny Aiello), who spends his jobless days with his cronies; her sole pleasure is going to the one and only cinema in her small New Jersey town and watching over and over again the films that are shown there.

The leading male character is the very epitome of a star, in fact, to be exact, he is a star. He is Tom Baxter (Jeff Daniels), 'explorer, adventurer and poet', a character from the film The Purple Rose of Cairo, shown in the local cinema. One fine evening, while Cecilia is watching the film for the umpteenth time, Tom Baxter notices her from the screen, then he steps down from it (literally) and runs away with the amazed girl, swearing his love for her. To Cecilia it does not seem to be true, but neither does it seem false. She now begins the strangest experience of her whole life. Although fearful, she does everything she can to make up some excuse to her husband so she can go out in the evening and meet her hero; she melts in his arms when he whispers sweet nothings in her ear. She does not even mind when her young man, incapable himself of distinguishing between real life and make-believe, tries to pay the bill in a restaurant with stage money, when he waits expectantly for a scene fade-out after he kisses Cecilia, or when he gets into a car and sits there, expecting it to start up by itself.

But the escape of a film character is an event which has consequences both on and off the screen. On the screen, the action is brought to a halt: the film cannot go on, and the other characters are forced to sit around, on comfortable sofas lent to them by the set designers, while they wait for something to happen. Meanwhile they have nothing better to do than bicker with the audience, who are left muttering angrily in the cinema. On this side of the screen, there is now the problem of recapturing a person who has never really existed, and who is wandering about New Jersey, capable of doing just about anything.

Other inconveniences are: the projector cannot be shut down, because then all the other characters would disappear and it would no longer be possible to put Tom Baxter back in his rightful place; the owner of the cinema is in danger of going bankrupt; the producer of the film has his money at risk also; while playing the part of Tom Baxter is a vain, ambitious actor called Gil Shepherd (Jeff Daniels again), who is running the risk of ruining his career.

And it is Gil Shepherd, along with the producer, who comes to the town to try and sort things out, and discovers Cecilia and her secret. Totally overwhelmed at finding herself in front of a real, flesh and blood Hollywood star, she takes Gil to meet his double, Tom Baxter. A big argument ensues, and each character comes away from it more firmly convinced of his own position than ever. Cecilia's husband is far more forthcoming. As soon as he manages to get his hands on Baxter, he beats him to a pulp. But Baxter is not even ruffled: as always happens in the cinema, after he has been beaten up, his hair is not even disarranged. Such are the advantages

Cecilia (Mia Farrow), a shy waitress, with her sister (Stephanie Farrow). She is ill-treated by her brutal husband, Monk (Danny Aiello).

of being make-believe. While the other Tom Baxters, projected in other cinemas across the States, begin to give signs of indiscipline, terrorising the producer, Gil Shepherd is busy courting Cecilia. He buys her a banjo, he showers her with compliments, and, all in all, he does everything possible to make himself even more attractive to her than the screen character he himself has brought to life. As for Tom Baxter, left momentarily to himself, he ends up in a brothel, where his gentle nature and noble spirit captivates all the girls. The only reason the situation does not develop into a full scale orgy is Tom's unwavering single-minded love for Cecilia.

Naturally, everything comes to a head. Tom is hounded, hungry and penniless. What can be done? One possible solution is to make the journey the other way round, i.e. take Cecilia inside the events of the film. Tom's work associates are more than willing. She is enthusiastic, and she passes a night the likes of which could only be lived in a film from the Thirties. Eventually, Tom and Gil come to a decisive confrontation. Gil asks Cecilia to make her choice, between a live actor and a made up character. With great regrets, Cecilia chooses the live actor. Tom Baxter returns to the film, and Cecilia goes home to pack her bags and run off with Gil. But Gil has tricked her and goes back to Hollywood, leaving her with her bags in her hands and her banjo (his present to her) under her arm. All that remains for her to do

Cecilia, who seeks refuge in a world of dreams, sees *The Purple Rose of Cairo* for the nth time.
The young star of the film (Jeff Daniels) leaves the screen and steps into her life.

is take refuge, yet again, in the cinema. She goes in to see Ginger Rogers and Fred Astaire dancing to the enchanting rhythms of Cheek To Cheek.

'If the critics don't like my film', Woody Allen said to the journalist Ron Base in February 1985, 'the public won't go to see it. And if the critics like it, that doesn't necessarily mean the public will go to see it.' The American critics did not give the public any clear, consistent message about *The Purple Rose of Cairo*. In favour of the film were Vincent Canby of *The New York Times*, Rex Reed of the *New York Post*; against were Todd McCarthy of *Variety*, William Wolf of the *Gannett News Service*, James Vernier of *Moviegoer*. Richard Schickel of *Time* was neutral. The selection of names is purely arbitrary, but does convey an idea of the opposing line-ups. As a consequence, the American audiences' attitude was not surprising: a lukewarm approval, of the type generally reserved for serious, but not major, works, by a director who is highly regarded. Things were different, however, in Europe, where the critics came out much more in favour of the film and

the public rushed to enjoy the tender story of a New Jersey Cinderella, for whom midnight strikes even before she has had the chance to having her first dance with the prince.

Without a doubt, the most important positive element of the film is the plot, with its intelligent combination of black and white film with colour film, of make-believe within reality. The ingeniously unreal device of making a character from fiction come to life derives from the re-working of an earlier story, *The Kugelmass Episode*, first published in the *New Yorker*, and later in the collection *Side Effects*. It tells the story of a visit, by a professor of literature from the City College of New York, to Madame Bovary in the novel, and then her return visit to New York. The story sparkled with intelligence and originality, but it did not contain any profound depths of meaning, nor any message. The film, on the other hand, aims also at being a philosphical and moral story, dealing with the problem of the relationship between illusion and reality, dreams and rationality. In this sense it is richer and more human, even if the conclusions it comes to, as we observe later on, are neither new or illuminating.

The editing of the film is also excellent. Without this time aiming at any daring formal solutions, Woody Allen confirms himself as someone of mature, sensitive imagination, and his camera (once again handled by his trusted director of photography, Gordon Willis) moves with all the smoothness and assurance of a major film-maker. The soundtrack is equally deserving of praise. Much could be written about its use of music. Nevertheless, it would be a mistake to over-rate *The Purple Rose*, which some people found 'perfect'.

In the end, the elegant little story of Cecilia and her celluloid love is no more than this: just a little story. *The Purple Rose* has the limitation of being based on one idea only: What would happen if a character from a film comes out of the film and sets foot amongst us? And then all the various possibilities, of comedy and plot, are thoroughly explored. As a consequence of this the film ends up by having no secret, unexplored areas, suggestions or echoes that the spectator can take out of the cinema with him, or discover at a later viewing. (In the story *The Kugelmass Episode* Woody Allen himself had written: 'The mark of a classic is that you can

reread it a thousand times and always find something new.' The remark was a cliché, used on this occasion for comic purposes, but it was also true, and it does not describe this film.) *Zelig* was as captivating and intriguing as a Chinese puzzle, a continual play of mirrors and reflections, and glimpses of things not easily grasped at first. *The Purple Rose*, on the other hand, is so crystal clear that it could almost be reduced to mathematical formulae: "Quod erat demonstrandum".

The slight story rests on slight characters. Cecilia is the second in a series of miniatures (in the sense of 'small portraits') of gentle victims of life, after *Broadway Danny Rose* in the film of the same name. The word 'series' is here used deliberately because one gets the impression that this Damon Runyon-like phase has become, if not a new chapter in Woody Allen's film-making, then certainly a vein of inspiration which is destined to continue in succeeding works. But while Danny Rose at least had quirks and contradictions which made him an intriguing character, the same cannot be said for Cecilia. Always she acts only 'consequentially', merely responding to circum-

stances and characters which dominate her life. In her voice, her facial expressions, all her actions, Mia Farrow once again demonstrates what an excellent actress she is, taking great pains to stay in character and not give in to the temptations of role playing. But Cecilia holds little dramatic interest: she is like a little bird, with no money, no determination and no foresight. It cannot really be said that the other characters are any more outstanding. The rough, coarse, selfish, insensitive husband (played enthusiastically by Danny Aiello) is a cardboard figure, predictable in everything he does. The actor, Gil Shepherd, aware of his charms and preoccupied with his career, is just as affected, a stereotype of a small time bad guy. Consequently the comedy of characters in which Woody Allen generally excels, fails to work here, and in its place we are left with the well oiled mechanism of situation comedy. And in such a comedy, since there is no need to make any deep examination of the characters, there is no opportunity to involve the audience in forming any views on the historical or social background against which the action takes place. As a result, any real feeling of the Thirties, a period of bright lights

and dark shadows, fails to come across, except perhaps in the long shots, as a set designer's aid: hovels, shut down factories, the unemployed, joyless streets. Allen could have gone into much greater depth if he had managed to maintain the hold he had shown in *Zelig*. The Roosevelt era, with its contrasts and hopes, would have been an excellent setting for a story-teller like him, with his love for historical and social mosaics.

The characteristic of the film on which most emphasis is placed is that of a philosophical tale. It is an enigmatic discourse on the cinema itself, on the imaginary, on make-believe, and the reverse. By a freak of logic, the cinema offers Cecilia the best possible lover. He is handsome, romantic, brave, faithful and passionate. Reality offers her, under the same appearance, a trickster who makes use of her to resolve his career problems. But it is to the cinema that Cecilia returns, to forget her sorrows in the rustlings of Ginger Rogers' dress and the brightness of Fred Astaire's smile. What are we supposed then to conclude about the cinema? Is it the opiate of the masses? The film gives no clear answers; in fact, it creates the impression of tickling the audience's

189

curiosity rather than seeking to stir the conscience. The pathetic elements, at the very end of the film, leave a definite bitter-sweet taste in the mouth. Moreover, a philosophical narrative should have a certain dramatic shape which is missing in this instance. There is no real collision between the two realities, inside and outside the film world. More play is made in each of them of incongruities in their logic: the fade-out that Tom awaits after the kiss, the lemonade that is served in place of champagne, the car which does not start up as soon as you sit in it, like it always does in the films, and so on. Buster Keaton's *The Cameraman*, which is often cited as an example, remains far superior in this field. In *The Cameraman*, the clash between the two realities becomes an epic of cinematographic expression, bewildering the perceptions.

If there is a moral to be drawn, it would seem to be the same as the one in the old *Sullivan's Travels* by Preston Sturges. We should allow celluloid dreams to exist because they serve as a balm for the wounds on the souls of simple people. Already conditioned by the movie-going fantasies, Cecilia falls in love with a non-existent person, then she falls into the arms of an actor who arrives by chance from the other side of the country; and a smile returns to her face when the images once again return to the screen. The cinema can trick people, but it can also soothe their pain.

To sum up, as we said earlier, one gets the impression that the film should be seen as a first-rate miniature, about little people who live through little events. But Woody Allen puts himself at risk when he attempts to create heroes out of the pallid characters in *The Purple Rose*. It was to be *Hannah And Her Sisters* which would lead him back to his true metier, showing human beings exactly as they are.

The acting deserves the highest praise. Mia Farrow, in a return to her earlier roles of the timid, virginal girl, is completely enchanting. With her voice, especially, she seems to be playing a sort of female version of one of the characters usually portrayed by Woody Allen himself. Jeff Daniels, whose only previous role of any importance had been that of the husband of Debra Winger in *Terms of Endearment*, found himself turned into a star by *The Purple Rose*: praise from the critics, female fans fainting before him, and a host of interviewers clamouring for his attention.

A search for references, or even just similarities with other films, leads us to *Sherlock Junior*, *Sullivan's Travels*, mentioned earlier, and then to *Pennies from Heaven*, to *Hellzapoppin* and *Lo Sceicco Bianco* by Fellini. We should end this piece with a quote from the film: 'I've met the most wonderful man', sighs Mia Farrow. 'Of course, he's fictional – but you can't have everything.' This is the most famous line from *The Purple Rose* – but it is taken straight out of *Some Like It Hot*. 'No-one is perfect', comments Joe E. Brown when he discovers the woman he loves is . . . Jack Lemmon.

Hannah And Her Sisters

'God, she's beautiful!' With this remark, in the midst of things, the film begins. There at once follows a close-up of Lee (Barbara Hershey), whose love-affair with Eliot (Michael Caine) is one of the main elements in the storyline. Lee is a former alcoholic, who has regained her equilibrium by getting together with Frederick (Max Von Sydow), an artist much older than she is. Eliot is a successful financial consultant who is married to Lee's sister Hannah, the Hannah of the title (Mia Farrow). The first scene, in which we see Eliot's shy and clumsy attempt at courting Lee, takes place in the house he lives in with Hannah, during the celebrations for Thanksgiving. The whole family is reunited: Eliot, Hannah and Lee, the third sister Holly (Dianne Wiest), the parents (Lloyd Nolan and Mia Farrow's real-life mother, Maureen O'Sullivan), other relatives and various friends. The parents are two retired musical-comedy entertainers who bask in their memories of a past that brought them to the brink of great successes but never to real success itself. The father likes to sit down at the piano and sing songs from the Thirties, the mother to reminisce about the beauty she once possessed. Holly shares all of Lee's weaknesses, and what is more, she has never succeeded in finding something on which to base her life. Having tried cocaine and succeeded in giving it up, she has formed an unrealistic ambition to become an actress, and goes from audition to audition in the hope of establishing herself. Her companion in her adventures is April (Carrie Fisher), a friend with markedly greater determination. Involved in this family story, as a lateral element, are the fortunes of Mickey Sachs (Woody Allen), Hannah's ex-husband, television producer and complete hypochondriac. Mickey's normal working day is frenetic, plagued by endless problems, caused by capricious actors, television censorship, and by many other things; but his real problem, which we find him confronting at the moment we first see him, is a slight loss of hearing in one ear. Naturally, he rushes to the doctor who, after making an exhaustive examination of his patient, recommends further tests. Fear becomes reality and then panic sets in when the X-ray results reveal a grey area on the cranium.

In the meantime, Eliot has managed to devise a strategy for continuing his courtship of Lee. He bumps into her 'by chance' outside her house and asks her to accompany him to a bookshop. Once there, he buys her a book, a collection of poems by E. E. Cummings, and directs her attention to a love poem 'on page 112', that had made him think of her when he himself had read it.

As for Holly, she, together with April, meets a handsome architect (Sam Waterston). At first the man seems to be more interested in April; but it is Holly who is invited to the opera at the Metropolitan; but at the end, it is once again April who gets the upper hand. As a consequence their friendship breaks up. Hannah, too, is at the centre of break-ups, either imminent or possible. Her marriage with Eliot is strained. Not simply on account of his infatuation with Lee, but, above all, because Hannah is 'perfect'. A talented and successful actress, she has given up her career for the joys of domesticity, and she has organised everything so well in family life that it functions like clockwork. In the beginning her husband had been reassured by such efficiency, but slowly he had begun to feel the distance between himself and his wife grow enormous. How can one live with a person to whom one can give nothing, a person who is simply perfect? Holly, too, finds much the same problem. She is always ready to turn to Hannah for her support or for a loan, but she is equally ready to criticise Hannah's lack of real communication and the pride, masked as generous humility, with which she behaves. Hannah, who is completely sincere in her relationships with the people she loves, does not take all this in, and goes on as before helping her sister on the next stage of her search for herself. In fact, Holly now wants to abandon her career as an actress and become a writer.

Crisis point is reached on the night of celebration of the next Thanksgiving Day, when Hannah, having read Holly's manuscript, accuses her of having spied on Hannah's married life and having gathered intimate details from her husband. The manuscript is full of extremely accurate extracts from conversations she has had with Eliot. In reality, it is Lee who, from time to time, has confided in Holly. She and Eliot have, in fact, become lovers and he understandably shares his domestic problems with her. The blaze of love between them was ignited at the home of Lee and Frederick, when Eliot brought a potential buyer to look at Frederick's paintings. While Frederick and the Buyer are in the cellar examining the works of art, Eliot takes his courage in his hands and rushes to kiss Lee. There follows a breathless, laboured declaration of love, first in the house and then in the street. For her part, Lee admits that she too feels something. The end result, amid guilt complexes about Frederick and Hannah, is an appointment in a hotel room,

The three sisters; the perfect wife, Hannah (Mia Farrow); the ex-alcoholic, Lee (Barbara Hershey); and the aspiring actress, Holly (Dianne Wiest).

which is followed by Lee breaking off her relationship with Frederick.

In the meantime, Mickey Sachs, the 'malade imaginaire', continues to have problems. After the unbearable strain of awaiting the results of the examination, his cloud of fear is finally dissolved: his brain is perfectly healthy and there is no trace of a tumour. But it is here that the worry really starts: even if, on this occasion, he has regained his health and life goes on, sooner or later something terrible will take place and it is therefore essential to find out if there is an afterlife. Thus begins the sad odyssey of a television director in search of eternal truth. Why not become a Catholic? No sooner said than done. But Catholicism is not enough and, what is

more, it drives his parents to despair (they are Jewish). What about Buddhism, then, since it preaches the doctrine of reincarnation? Buddhism is not what he is looking for either. Nothing remains but for him to take his own life; but the sweat on his forehead causes the barrel of the weapon to slip and the only thing that gets shot is a mirror. Once again we have to turn to the Marx Brothers to resolve matters. In the grip of the blackest depression, Mickey wanders around the upper East Side until, looking only for somewhere to rest, he goes into a cinema. Duck Soup is being shown. As if by magic, Mickey discovers a philosophy of good sense: he doesn't know if God exists, but equally, he doesn't know that God does not exist; as long as he is alive there is the possibility of enjoying himself; there will be plenty of time to kill himself tomorrow. When by chance he meets Holly in a record shop, he amuses her with his jokes and

ends up reading one of her manuscripts, which is very good. Thus begins the love-story between Mickey and Holly, which had been half started years earlier when Hannah, divorced from Mickey, had introduced him to her sister, who was always in search of eligible bachelors.

Relationships move towards their final arrangement. The friction between Hannah and Eliot is resolved by Hannah's acknowledgement of her own weaknesses; and this, together with the genuine love that her husband feels for her, holds their marriage together. Lee becomes attached to a university lecturer whom she meets while attempting to follow some course of study. Even the elderly parents manage to quarrel and make up, the cause being the mother's habit, despite her years, of flirting. In this way, another Thanksgiving Day comes around: everyone is happy, but happiest of all are Mickey and Holly, now married. And as a final note of

193

(Left) Lee and her artist lover, Frederick (Max Von Sydow), discuss his paintings with a potential buyer (Daniel Stern), brought to the house by Eliot (Michael Caine).
(Left, below) The girls' parents (Lloyd Nolan and Maureen O'Sullivan, Mia Farrow's real-life mother) entertain their grandchildren.
(Right) In spite of his infidelity with Lee, the end of the film sees Eliot reunited with his wife, Hannah (Mia Farrow).

joy, Holly announces her big news: she is expecting a baby. Mickey, who had been diagnosed as sterile, is over the moon.

Hannah And Her Sisters signals a step backwards in the evolution of Woody Allen as far as the themes are concerned on which his inspiration is based. The inspiration of his recent films had been the precept that 'small is beautiful': the little man who becomes famous because he has the characteristics of the chameleon (*Zelig*), the little theatrical agent who is a kindly loser (*Broadway Danny Rose*), and the small, gentle provincial soul who takes refuge in a world of cinematic dreams (*The Purple Rose of Cairo*). Here, in *Hannah And Her Sisters*, Allen goes more directly back to the powerful vein that inspired *Annie Hall* and *Manhattan* (and if we choose to include it, also *Interiors*): descriptions of real people in this day and age, with their rages and their tensions, their imperfections and their foolishness. The subtlety and tenderness with which Allen is gifted allows him to portray everyday life with a light touch which is at times almost sparkling. He is able to transform a story of amorous intrigues, jealousy, spite, rancour and existential verbiage into a harmonious, interwoven piece, full of

affection for the characters, for the place in which they live and for the things that they do. This is Woody Allen's remarkable achievement. We should ask ourselves if any other script writer/director could have allowed himself to have one of his actresses remark 'It is such a black night. I feel lost', without arousing outbursts of scornful laughter in the cinema? Or could have portrayed a character who is for months on the verge of suicide, and then sorts out his life by going to see a Marx Brothers film? Could any other director have made the same character express the maxims of bourgeois common sense as if they were the most elevated thoughts? Intellectuals, who have always made up the core of the New York director's following, ought by rights to shudder because of their characteristic scepticism. But, on the contrary, they applaud.

There is a wise old saying which states: between the sublime and the ridiculous there is the width of a razor-blade. Once again we can probably learn something from Woody Allen about comedy which is just the opposite of ridiculous. Mickey Sachs is clearly a comic character. He is even a re-working of a stock character from European comedy, the *Malade Imaginaire* of Molière. Now, the comic is

comical because it is *exaggerated* as well as being incongruous. Something which is merely incongrous, not exaggerated but *reduced*, debased, becomes instead ridiculous. The right mixture between these elements is very difficult to achieve.

Mickey, with his exaggerated fears and his exaggerated nonconformity, finds an answer which is of equally inflated banality. Basically, he discovers a truth which the entire human race already knows. But the discovery is not ridiculous and neither is Mickey Sachs. And since the comedy is engaging and not alienating, truthful and not short-sighted, so Mickey Sachs' message of truth comes across to the spectator as something genuine, from one human being to another: there is hope, I have come across it.

The main fault in this otherwise almost perfect film is an excess of wordiness and elaboration. The characters talk incessantly, and often they do this instead of allowing the spectator to deduce their various characters from their actions and behaviour. Hannah, for example, does absolutely nothing to demonstrate that she is 'the top of the class', which is how she is described and is also how she defines herself. The painter, Frederick, is little more than a mask,

195

and it is the dialogue which informs us so much about his work, his points of view, and the type of relationship he has with Lee. This aspect sometimes causes us to feel a sense of premeditation, as if the whole film were somehow remote-controlled, despite its apparent spontaneity.

The charm of *Hannah* lies in the attempt (successful about eighty per cent of the time) to adjust correctly the mixture between material which is on the one hand as informal, everyday and documentary as possible, and on the other hand a structure which is rigorous and fixed. The stories of the different characters criss-cross continuously (demonstrating Allen's absolutely impeccable mastery of film editing), and they move along, with one giving way to the next, without ever lapsing into digression or irrelevance (Mickey's eschatological course is, it seems, kept to one side, but essentially it provides an indis-

pensable balance to the very egotistical events in the others' lives). The narration itself is confined by three Thanksgiving Day parties, one of which takes place at the start, one at the end, and one in the middle of the film. The human relationships between the various individuals can be looked at as two triangles with a single vertex – Hannah: she has two sisters and two husbands, one divorced and one current; each of the two husbands has a love-affair with one of the sisters.

What actually takes place is, on the other hand, very mundane. Nothing in the narrative is made spectacular. Little stories of love – or the search for love, of work or the search for work, of fears and anxieties, and of minor vexations. The careful depiction of the middle class and the lower middle-classes of New York. The poetry lies in the truth.

It has been said that *Hannah* is

Manhattan in colour. In part this is true, and as far as the artistic value of this film is concerned, it is certainly very close to what was, and remains, Woody Allen's best work. In *Hannah*, too, the city itself is again among the protagonists, impressing throughout with the beauty of its architecture and the colours of the East River and Central Park. As in *Manhattan* the film exudes tenderness and sensitivity, indulgence and fragility. And even more than *Manhattan*, which ends with the famous remark by Tracey to Ike, 'You have to have a little faith in people', *Hannah* breathes with hope and love for life. It is not by chance that the film ends with the announcement that Holly is expecting a baby and that the sterility which had undermined Mickey's previous marriage is a thing of the past. The arc of the film is of a journey from uncertainty to certainty, from compromise to sincerity: at the end of it, Lee, Holly

196

(Left) Holly's friend, April (Carrie Fisher), shares a laugh at a party with the handsome architect (Sam Waterston).

(Below) The hypochondriac TV producer, Mickey Sachs (Woody Allen), talks with his ex-wife, Hannah (Mia Farrow).

and Mickey are happily married, Hannah and Eliot have recovered their harmony together and the parents go on, in their own way, sustaining their own relationship. The whole film seems to be an affirmative response to the invitation contained in that last remark made in *Manhattan*.

As far as style is concerned, the novelty is obvious enough. For the first time, Allen is not looking out for the beautiful frame, nor seeking to display his cinematic virtuosity. Leaving the camera in the hands of Antonioni's ex-director of photography, Carlo Di Palma, Allen has also assented to an almost documentary-style use of the dolly (i.e. at the beginning the methodical close-up, then move the dolly backwards to reveal the setting – this is repeated four or five times), looking for the poetry of the invisible camera, a straightforward witness to events.

This casual attitude is perfect for the chosen photographic ends, where warm tones predominate (and in the printing process the dominant red was even accentuated). Already a great portrait painter, of Ravenna in *Red Desert*, and London in *Blow-Up*, Di Palma excels himself with his caressing panoramas of the sights of Manhattan. The actors, too, owe him a great deal. The ability of Di Palma and Allen, to extract from the faces and gestures of the three female leads every shade, every heaviness of the eyes and every tremor of the lips, is worthy of Bergman at his best. Barbara Hershey benefits from this in particular in her first really worthwhile part after a career spanning more than fifteen years, and so does Dianne Wiest, in her turn discovered by the cinema (she had had a small part as a prostitute in *The Purple Rose of Cairo*) after a long and successful

career in the theatre. Allen, like Bergman, is very good at female characters. A female critic has rightly remarked that he is, in reality, the only American director who likes women: *they please him*, they don't arouse him or push him to idealisations: In practice, Allen's human and intellectual sympathies are always with women, as he himself has stated in more than one interview; if I have to deal with serious themes, Allen has said, I prefer to do so using female characters. Nevertheless, the male characters are no less successful: we only have to think of Eliot, into whom Michael Caine puts all those uncharacteristic qualities that he had never had the chance of manifesting in more than twenty years work as an actor; or, obviously, Mickey Sachs, the character played by Allen himself.

Lastly, the highest praise should go to Jeffrey Kurland for the costumes.

197

Radio Days

Set in Rockaway (Queens, New York) at the outset of World War II, Radio Days *invites the audience to partake in the hilarious yet moving adventures of a family, whose members triumph over a mundane existence by cultivating an intense fantasy life. Like Woody Allen's previous film,* Hannah And Her Sisters, *this is also a family saga. The joys and tribulations experienced by all – parents and children, uncles and aunts, neighbours and friends – are universally recognisable: an unmarried aunt craves the company of a prince charming who remains ever-elusive; a wife lingers lovingly on the memory of a previous courtship; a boy accepts the Masked Avenger, the famous radio character, as part and parcel of his daily life; a man believes his get rich schemes will bring him the success he has never had. But even if the nature of dreams precludes most from coming true, the very fact that the characters of* Radio Days *choose to confront, and be inspired by, them lends them an almost heroic dimension.*

Radio Days also offers a glance at the active Manhattan night-life, where the rich and beautiful rub elbows with other dreamers. Amidst the cigarette smoke, champagne and big band music, a charming but none-too-bright cigarette girl will become a radio personality, actually fulfilling her ambition.*

Radio Days is essentially a film without a plot, made up of a number of different episodes with a variety of facets. In some ways, because of its structure, the film calls to mind Woody Allen's early 'formless comedies', like *Take The Money And Run*, although *Radio Days* lacks the narrative backbone of this film. The American critics, who always pay great attention to someone who has become, over the years, the country's most stimulating film-maker, were just about evenly divided about this one. Rather than expressing the author's judgement of criticisms, it is worth taking the space to offer the panorama of reactions from the American critics.

The first, and most clear-cut, difference of opinion concerned Woody Allen's attitude towards the subject he is dealing with. Normally, everyone had their own memories of childhood and adolescence, and, throughout our lives, these are generally memories that we cherish dearly. Here are two completely opposite reactions from two journalists and writers. Vincent Canby, of the *New York Times*, wrote 'For most of us who were born before World War II – or even during the war's early days – it is sometimes difficult to realise that these extraordinary objects are now antiques, and that the material that poured from their speakers constituted a singular, if short-lived, popular art. We didn't have to look at the radio – though we always did – to be swept up by the voice of the unkown diva on *The Major Bowes Amateur Hour*, the awful dooms facing *Little Orphan Annie*, the arcane knowledge possessed by contestants on *Name That Tune*, the adventures of *The Lone Ranger*, or the gaiety of the annual New Year's Eve festivies at the Roosevelt Hotel, presided over by Guy Lombardo. We didn't see a wooden cabinet, often scratched and scuffed, its speaker fabric punctured by children who'd wanted to discover what was going on inside.

'Instead we saw a limitless universe, created entirely out of voices, music and sound effects, that liberated each mind in direct relation to the quality of its imagination. Radio wasn't outside our lives. It coincided with – and helped to shape – our childhood and adolescence. As we slogged towards maturity, it also grew up and turned into television, leaving behind like dead skin, transistorised talk-radio and non-stop music shows.'

His conclusion is this: 'At this point I can't think of any film-maker of Mr Allen's generation with whom he can be compared, certainly no-one at work in American movies today. As the writer, director and star (even when he doesn't actually appear) of his films, Mr Allen works more like a novelist who's able to pursue his own obsessions, fantasies and concerns without improvements imposed on him by committees. At this point, too, his films can be seen as part of a rare continuum. Each of us has his favourite Allen movie, but to cite one over another as 'more important,' 'bigger,' 'smaller' or 'less significant' is to miss the joys of the entire body of work that is now taking shape. *Radio Days* is a joyful addition. Mr Allen, our most prodigal cinema resource, moves on.'

And here is the opposite reaction from Gerald Nachman, of the *San Francisco Chronicle*: 'As a radio maniac, I looked forward to the film and was terribly dismayed I didn't love it more, as much as I loved radio. It bothered me that Allen didn't do it more justice. The love is there but I felt he was trading more on the public memory than his own, a kind of received nostalgia, a trivia game. That shared memory, as depicted in *Radio Days*, is threadbare by now, conventional and unconvincing. We know it too well by heart, at least those of my dotage. I suspect if you're too young to have lived it, the movie works better. As one who did, *Radio Days* is

Diane Keaton plays a cameo role in this film, which is made up of a number of different episodes, each filled with the music and the flavour of those 'golden days' of the past.

only an approximation and, for all its sentiment, didn't convey to me what it was like to be transfixed by radio's transcendent powers. Everybody has his own memories, which is why radio had such a hold on us. *Radio Days* has too many stock memories and not enough unique ones. It doesn't recall old radio so much as old memories.'

So much for the subject. Mike Clark, of the popular daily *USA Today*, also placed the emphasis on the subject matter: 'The predominant theme – and you should keep this in mind – is . . . radio days. Keep it in mind because I'm guessing there'll be some who will tell you that Allen substitutes vignettes for a conventional orderly script – or that the two halves of his story never mesh. What nonsense.

'You exit this extraordinary mood piece knowing something of how the medium worked, about the effect of then-new mass communication on hitherto provincial lives, and of the now obscure personalities who once entered our homes more frequently than the milkman.'

A safe prophecy. For Stephen Hunter, the cinema critic of the *Sun*, observed: 'Gertrude Stein once pointed out to Ernest Hemingway that remarks are not literature. Slightly updated, that verdict must be directed at Woody Allen: Remarks are not movies, either.

'Allen's new film, *Radio Days*, has the feel of a series of remarks rather than a series of stories: it's just uttered. It strives to recreate his childhood worship of the radio and that

instrument's larger impact on the culture, but, although pleasant and occasionally amusing, the film is so thin and sketchy it qualifies as a major disappointment. The movie also shuffles disconsolately through a number of slightly fictionalised golden radio moments, such as Orson Welles' mock-documentary of a Martian invasion in New Jersey. In this respect, it's more like a diorama than a drama.

'If all this were convulsively funny or if some other emotion dominated,

there wouldn't be any problem. But far more typically the humour misfires, and the little stories pop like soap bubbles as they reach their climax, leaving us muddled and displeased.'

Michael Sauter, in *Nightlife*, pointed out that this jumping from one subject to another, did, at least, have precedents: 'Indeed the whole movie plays like a full-length *Annie Hall* flashback, one that has not only been extended, but also expanded,

199

(Left) A picture of a happy family, (bottom row, left to right) William Magerman, Seth Green, Leah Carey; (top row, left to right) Michael Tucker, Julie Kavner, Dianne Wiest, Joy Newman, Renée Lippin and Josh Mostel. (Left, below) Although they lead a modest life, the husband and wife (Michael Tucker and Julie Kavner) are made happy by the world of bright dreams which radio inspires. (Right) Tony Roberts and Dianne Wiest in front of the radio microphone, the omnipresent protagonist in the film.

deepened and enriched, with more textures, more meanings, fuller comic characters.'

Andrew Sarris, the prophet of the 'politique des auteurs', who gives forth from the pulpit of the much revered *Village Voice*, noted: '*Radio Days* works for me precisely because it is so lightly sketched, and because it does not cheat on historical hindsights. Where Allen is more in tune with the zeitgeist is in his broadening of his formulas into absurdist farce. He takes everything that is dangerously nostalgic and sentimental too far, not for the sake of a self-conscious snicker, nor even for an indulgent smile, but simply for the syncopated pathos of an ever wandering mind slowly evolving into an inimitably personal style.'

With Sarris, we reach the more specific criticisms of the film. In *Newsweek*, David Ansen's view was positive: 'It's a film only Woody Allen could have made, and given the current state of daring among producers, a film only he could have gotten away with making. More power to him. Though in some ways it's only an elaborate doodle – a minor work in the Allen canon – it's nice to report that Woody remains oblivious to the pressure to repeat his former successes. *Radio Days* turns its back to genre and to any claims to Importance. What you see is what you get.'

The reaction of David Thomson, of the *California Magazine*, was also positive: '*Radio Days* seems to me a great deal better than *Hannah* as well as bolder, more innovative and more assured than anything Woody Allen has ever done. There's not an Amer-

ican career for which we can hold higher hopes. By the time he's say, 65, he might be really something, a little old artist, poised between coldness and sentiment, and giving up that riddle for the fascination of a dementedly imaginative and imaginary America. For as time goes by, it becomes clearer that Allen is surrendering self-concern so that America and its self-awareness can be his subjects. No other director is more fitted for the heritage of *Citizen Kane* and Orson Welles.'

Also in favour, but with reservations, was James Verniere of the *Boston Globe*: '*Radio Days*, like *The Purple Rose of Cairo*, is delicious and light-hearted, two virtues in short supply in most films. It's also marvellously, almost luxuriously, paced and acted. And it's obviously a 'personal' film, focussing in part on a boy named Joe (Seth Green), who – like Woody Allen – came of age in Brooklyn around the time of World War II. But like *Purple Rose*, *Radio Days* is also a confection: a spun-sugar tribute to innocence, romance and popular entertainment. And in the end, it's the kind of film that leaves the viewer with the queasy sensation that he's had dessert, but no meal. It's an incan-

tory mix of sight and sound, of the music and the showbiz personalities who provided real people with the stuff of hopes and dreams. But in the end, the spirits Woody Allen summons up in *Radio Days* melt in thin air the minute we leave the theatre.'

There are also those critics who have seized the opportunity to indulge in a much deeper analysis rather than just express a simple judgement on this one specific film. For example, Larry Swindell wrote in the *Star-Telegram*: Someday Woody Allen will make a great motion picture, and the day may be soon. He's getting closer to the shrine. *Radio Days* is his most protean and ambitious work. He is a superb motion picture director. The new film has a marvellous visual character; it is shrewdly observed and cannily framed, with a richness of detail in its images that is especially gratifying in a period piece. Allen is incrementally winning the struggle to find the right form, the right style for what I would call his genius. Woody Allen is really the Charles Dickens of American cinema and my hunch is that *Radio Days* is Woody's *David Copperfield*.'

The attitude of John Podhoretz, writing in *Insight*, could not have been

The contrasting lifestyles of two couples. (Left) The heedless nightlife of Manhattan (David Warrilow and Mia Farrow), and (below) the realities of family life (Leah Carey and William Magerman).

more different: 'Woody Allen, who is probably the most celebrated American director now at work, reveals again that his film-making vocabulary is too limited and pretentious. *Radio Days* is an American version of Fellini's *Amarcord*. With the exception of *Annie Hall*, all his films after *Love And Death* have suffered from the Art disease. 'When a director dies', said a great documentarian John Grierson, 'he becomes a photographer'. As a servant of Art, then, Allen is becoming more and more estranged from his greatest gift: to crack intelligent jokes for intelligent people.'

Almost as a deliberate reply, here is what Geoffrey Himes wrote in the *Columbia Flier*: 'Best of all, this film is genuinely funny. Because it is obviously such a lightweight film, Allen apparently feels free to indulge his old knack for slapstick comedy and ethnic humour. Whether describing Uncle Abe's encounter with the Communists next door or a sportscaster's description of a blind, amputee baseball pitcher, some of these vignettes are side-splittingly funny. Artistry is not the product of weighty subjects or profound messages: it comes from an ability to get into the dark corners of life as it is actually lived and turn on the lights without knocking over any of the furniture. Even in a film as slight as *Radio Days*, Woody Allen's artistry is unmistakable.'

Other commentators point out instead the subtle message of the film. Here, for example, is the analysis of Julie Salaman, of the *Wall Street Journal*: 'Mr Allen returns here to one of his basic themes – the influence of popular fantasy on his life and his art. Remember, this is a man who had the hero of *Hannah And Her Sisters* find redemption at a Marx Brothers movie.

In *The Purple Rose of Cairo*, he was even blunter about the importance of the pop culture of his youth. The only life worth living, the film suggested, was life lived on film.'

In complete contrast, David Denby, of the *New York* magazine, stated: 'Woody Allen's idea seems to be that radio, which appealed to people's imagination and their love of romance and story-telling, brought everyone together. Yet the scenes of togetherness in *Radio Days* give us very little to cheer about. At the end of the *Purple Rose of Cairo*, the movie dreamers were left with nothing in their lives – nothing but dreams. The same is almost true of the radio listeners here. And the celebrities, enjoying their New Year's Eve champagne on a Times Square rooftop, are headed for an obscurity just as profound as the one blanketing the poor Jewish families of Rockaway. Why is the movie so sad and muffled? Perhaps because, deep down, Woody Allen realises that radio and movies aren't enough. Yet he can't bear that idea, so these reminiscences of popular culture in his youth get dragged down by the bad thoughts he's suppressing.'

Finally, here is the reaction of Sheila Benson, from the columns of the *Los Angeles Times*: 'In retrospect, *Radio Days* takes on a deeper resonance, a suggestion that these memories, both pure and shamelessly exaggerated, aren't trivial but the absolute stuff of life, to be collected as seriously as war bonds. There is a tender sense of the mature artist, pinning down the ephemeral with the greatest care – letting us know how it felt in 1944 to greet the New Year from a Times Square rooftop, dwarfed by gigantic advertising signs, with a light snow

beginning to fall on bare shoulders and dinner jackets.'

Wholehearted praise is reserved for the various members of the cast. Michael Sauter, in *Nightlife*, wrote: 'Allen's evocation of radio days is the triumph of a unique artistic vision. But by no means is it his alone. Also contributing brilliantly is his regular team of collaborators: Santo Loquasto with his sets that range from a homey living-room to a ritzy ballroom to a rooftop overlooking Times Square; Jeffrey Kurland, whose costumes seem to have sprung from the pages of *Live* magazine circa 1940; Carlo Di Palma, whose cinematography casts them all in a perfect period light; and Dick Hyman whose assemblage of vintage jazz and pop tunes forms a continuous musical backdrop – a soundtrack big and generous enough to include Glenn Miller and Kurt Weill, Cole Porter and Carmen Miranda, *Flight of The Bumblebee* and *Mairzy Doats*. Truly everyone memorable here, everyone irreplaceable: just as every period prop, sound-effect, image and insight contributes invaluably to the richness – and rightness – of this re-invented world.'

Susan Stark, of the *Detroit News*, concluded her penetrating comment on the film with a phrase that can also be used to end this parade of views and opinions: 'In the long run, *Radio Days* will no doubt assume secondary status in consideration of the films of Woody Allen. It lacks both the structural integrity and refinement of his most important films. In some ways, though, examining the sketchbook can be as enjoyable and edifying as looking at the full-blown masterpiece.'

FILMS

(*indicates films which were not directed by Woody Allen)

1965 WHAT'S NEW, PUSSYCAT?*
DIRECTOR: Clive Donner;
SCREENPLAY: Woody Allen;
PHOTOGRAPHY: Jean Badal
(Technicolor, Scope); ART
DIRECTOR: Jacques Saulnier;
MUSIC: Burt Bacharach; EDITOR:
Fergus McDonnell; PRODUCTION:
Charles K. Feldman – Famous Artists
CAST: Peter Sellers (Fritz
Fassbender), Peter O'Toole (Michael
James), Romy Schneider (Carol
Werner), Capucine (Renée
Lefebvre), Ursula Andress (Rita),
Paula Prentiss (Liza Bien), Woody
Allen (Victor Shakapopolis)
RUNNING TIME: 120 minutes

1966 WHAT'S UP, TIGER LILY?*
Title of the original Japanese version:
KAGI NO KAGI (literal
translation: THE KEY OF KEYS)
DIRECTOR: Senkichi Taniguchi;
SCREENPLAY: Hideo Ando;
PHOTOGRAPHY: Kazuo Yamada
(Eastmancolor, Scope);
PRODUCTION: Tomoyuki Tanaka
for Toho; AMERICAN VERSION:
EXECUTIVE PRODUCER: Henry
G. Saperstein; DIRECTOR OF THE
ADDED SCENES AND
DIALOGUES: Woody Allen;
PRODUCTION: Ben Shapiro;
EDITOR: Richard Krown;
DUBBING: Woody Allen, Frank
Buxton, Len Maxwell, Louise
Lasser, Mickey Rose, Julie Bennett,
Bryna Wilson; MUSIC: The Lovin'
Spoonful
CAST: Tatsuta Mihashi (Phil
Moskowitz), Mihi Hana (Terry
Yaki), Eiko Wakayabayashi (Suki
Yaki), Tadao Nakamaru (Shepherd
Wong), Susumu Kurobe (Wing Fat)
RUNNING TIME: 79 minutes

1967 CASINO ROYALE*
DIRECTORS: John Huston, Kenneth
Hughes, Val Guest, Robert Parrish,
Joseph McGrath; SUBJECT: From
the novel by Ian Fleming;
SCREENPLAY: Wolf Mankowitz,
John Law, Michael Sayers;
PHOTOGRAPHY: Jack Hildyard
(Technicolor, Panavision); ART
DIRECTOR: Michael Ayringer;
MUSIC: Burt Bacharach; EDITOR:
Bill Lenny; PRODUCTION: Charles
K. Feldman – Famous Artists
CAST: Peter Sellers (Evelyn
Tremble), Ursula Andress (Vesper
Lynd), David Niven (James Bond),
Orson Welles (Le Chiffre), Joanna
Pettet (Mata Bond), Woody Allen

(Jimmy Bond)
RUNNING TIME: 131 minutes

**1969 DON'T DRINK THE
WATER***
DIRECTOR: Howard Morris;
SUBJECT: From the play by Woody
Allen; SCREENPLAY: R.S. Allen
and Harvey Bullock;
PHOTOGRAPHY: Harvey Genkins
(Colour by Berkey Pathé); ART
DIRECTOR: Robert Gundlach;
MUSIC: Pat Williams; EDITOR:
Ralph Rosenblum; PRODUCTION:
Charles H. Joffe
CAST: Jackie Gleason (Walter
Hollander), Estelle Parsons (Marion
Hollander), Ted Bessel (Axel Magee),
Joan Delaney (Susan Hollander),
Richard Libertini (Father Drobny)
RUNNING TIME: 98 minutes

1969 TAKE THE MONEY AND RUN
DIRECTOR: Woody Allen; SUBJECT
AND SCREENPLAY: Woody Allen
and Mickey Rose;
PHOTOGRAPHY: Lester Schorr
(Technicolor); ART DIRECTOR:
Fred Harpman; MUSIC: Marvin
Hamlisch; EDITORS: Paul Jordon,
Ron Kalish, Ralph Rosenblum;
PRODUCTION: Charles H. Joffe –
Palomar Pictures
CAST: Woody Allen (Virgil
Starkwell), Janet Margolin (Louise),
Marcel Hillaire (Fritz), Jacqueline
Hyde (Miss Blair), Lonnie Chapman
(Jake)
RUNNING TIME: 85 minutes

1971 BANANAS
DIRECTOR: Woody Allen;
SUBJECT AND SCREENPLAY:
Woody Allen and Mickey Rose;
PHOTOGRAPHY: Andrew M.
Kostikyan (Deluxe Color); ART
DIRECTOR: Ed Wittstein; MUSIC:
Marvin Hamlisch; PRODUCTION:
Jack Grossberg – Rollins and Joffe –
United Artists
CAST: Woody Allen (Fielding
Mellish), Louise Lasser (Nancy)
Carlos Montalban (Vargas), Jacobo
Morales (Esposito), Natividad
Abascal (Yolanda), Howard Cosell
(himself)
RUNNING TIME: 81 minutes

1972 PLAY IT AGAIN, SAM*
DIRECTOR: Herbert Ross;
SUBJECT AND SCREENPLAY:
Woody Allen, from his own play;
PHOTOGRAPHY: Owen Roizman
(Technicolor); ART DIRECTOR: Ed
Wittstein; MUSIC: Billy
Goldenberg; EDITOR: Marion
Rothman; PRODUCTION: Charles
H. Joffe – Frank Capra Jr. – Apjac/
Paramount

CAST: Woody Allen (Allan Felix),
Diane Keaton (Linda Christie), Tony
Roberts (Dick Christie), Jerry Lacy
(Humphrey Bogart), Susan Anspach
(Nancy)
RUNNING TIME: 84 minutes

**1972 EVERYTHING YOU
ALWAYS WANTED TO KNOW
ABOUT SEX BUT WERE AFRAID
TO ASK**
DIRECTOR: Woody Allen;
SUBJECT AND SCREENPLAY:
Woody Allen; PHOTOGRAPHY:
David M. Walsh (Deluxe Color);
ART DIRECTOR: Dale Hennesy;
MUSIC: Mundell Lowe; EDITOR:
Eric Albertson; PRODUCTION:
Charles H. Joffe – Jack Brodsky –
United Artists
CAST: Woody Allen (Clown,
Fabrizio, Victor, Sperm), Gene
Wilder (Dr Ross), John Carradine
(Dr Bernardo), Lou Jacobi (Sam),
Louise Lasser (Gina), Lynn Redgrave
(Queen), Anthony Quayle (King),
Burt Reynolds (Commander of the
Control Centre)
RUNNING TIME: 87 minutes

1973 SLEEPER
DIRECTOR: Woody Allen;
SUBJECT AND SCREENPLAY:
Woody Allen and Marshall
Brickman; PHOTOGRAPHY: David
M. Walsh (Deluxe Color); ART
DIRECTOR: Dale Hennesy; MUSIC:
Woody Allen; EDITOR: Ralph
Rosenblum; PRODUCTION: Jack
Grossberg – Rollins and Joffe –
United Artists
CAST: Woody Allen (Miles
Monroe), Diane Keaton (Luna), John
Beck (Erno) Mary Gregory (Dr Melik)
RUNNING TIME: 87 minutes

1975 LOVE AND DEATH
DIRECTOR: Woody Allen;
SUBJECT AND SCREENPLAY:
Woody Allen; PHOTOGRAPHY:
Ghislain Cloquet (DeLuxe color);
ART DIRECTOR: Willy Holt;
MUSIC: compositions by Sergei
Prokofiev; EDITORS: Ralph
Rosenblum, Ron Kalish;
PRODUCTION: Charles H. Joffe –
United Artists
CAST: Woody Allen (Boris
Grusenko), Diane Keaton (Sonia),
Olga Georges-Picot (Countess
Alexandrovna), Harold Gould (Count
Anton), Jessica Harper (Natasha)
James Tolkan (Napoleon)
RUNNING TIME: 85 minutes

1976 THE FRONT*
DIRECTOR: Martin Ritt; SUBJECT
AND SCREENPLAY: Martin Ritt
and Walter Bernstein;

PHOTOGRAPHY: Michael Chapman (Colour, Panavision); ART DIRECTOR: Charles Bailey; MUSIC: Dave Grusin; EDITOR: Sidney Levin; PRODUCTION: Martin Ritt – Rollins and Joffe – Columbia Pictures
CAST: Zero Mostel (Hecky Brown), Woody Allen (Howard Prince), Herschel Bernardi (Phil Sussman), Michael Murphy (Alfred Miller), Andrea Marcovicci (Florence Barrett), Remak Ramsay (Hennessey)
RUNNING TIME: 94 minutes

1977 ANNIE HALL
DIRECTOR: Woody Allen; SUBJECT AND SCREENPLAY: Woody Allen and Marshall Brickman; PHOTOGRAPHY: Gordon Willis (Panavision); ART DIRECTOR: Mel Bourne; MUSIC: songs from the repertoire; EDITOR: Ralph Rosenblum; PRODUCTION: Charles H. Joffe – United Artists
CAST: Woody Allen (Alvy Singer), Diane Keaton (Annie Hall), Tony Roberts (Rob), Carol Kane (Allison), Paul Simon (Tony Lacey), Shelley Duvall (Pam), Janet Margolin (Robin), Christopher Walken (Duane Hall)
RUNNING TIME: 93 minutes

1978 INTERIORS
DIRECTOR: Woody Allen; SUBJECT AND SCREENPLAY: Woody Allen; PHOTOGRAPHY: Gordon Willis (Colour); ART DIRECTOR: Mel Bourne; MUSIC: from the repertoire; EDITOR: Ralph Rosenblum; PRODUCTION: Charles H. Joffe – United Artists
CAST: Mary Beth Hurt (Joey), Diane Keaton (Renata), Kristin Griffith (Flyn), Geraldine Page (Eve), Maureen Stapleton (Pearl), E.G. Marshall (Arthur), Richard Jordan (Frederick), Sam Waterston (Mike)
RUNNING TIME: 93 minutes

1979 MANHATTAN
DIRECTOR: Woody Allen; SUBJECT AND SCREENPLAY: Woody Allen and Marshall Brickman; PHOTOGRAPHY: Gordon Willis (black and white); ART DIRECTOR: Mel Bourne; MUSIC: Compositions by George Gershwin; EDITOR: Susan E. Morse; PRODUCTION: Charles H. Joffe – United Artists
CAST: Woody Allen (Isaac Davis), Diane Keaton (Mary Wilke), Michael Murphy (Yale), Mariel Hemingway (Tracy), Meryl Streep (Jill), Anne Byrne (Emily)
RUNNING TIME: 96 minutes

1980 STARDUST MEMORIES
DIRECTOR: Woody Allen; SUBJECT AND SCREENPLAY: Woody Allen; PHOTOGRAPHY: Gordon Willis (black and white); ART DIRECTOR: Mel Bourne; MUSIC: songs from the repertoire; EDITOR: Susan E. Morse; PRODUCTION: Robert Greenhut – Rollins and Joffe – United Artists
CAST: Woody Allen (Sandy Bates), Charlotte Rampling (Dorrie), Jessica Harper (Daisy), Marie-Christine Barrault (Isobel), Tony Roberts (Tony)
RUNNING TIME: 89 minutes

1982 A MIDSUMMER NIGHT'S SEX COMEDY
DIRECTOR: Woody Allen; SUBJECT AND SCREENPLAY: Woody Allen; PHOTOGRAPHY: Gordon Willis (Technicolor, Panavision); ART DIRECTOR: Speed Hopkins; MUSIC: compositions by Felix Mendelssohn; EDITOR: Susan E. Morse; PRODUCTION: Robert Greenhut – Charles H. Joffe – Orion Pictures
CAST: Woody Allen (Andrew), Mia Farrow (Ariel), José Ferrer (Leopold), Tony Roberts (Maxwell), Mary Steenburgen (Adrian), Julie Hagerty (Dulcy)
RUNNING TIME: 94 minutes

1983 ZELIG
DIRECTOR: Woody Allen; SUBJECT AND SCREENPLAY: Woody Allen; PHOTOGRAPHY: Gordon Willis (Black and white/colour); ART DIRECTOR: Mel Bourne; MUSIC: songs composed and adapted by Dick Hyman, and songs from the repertoire; EDITOR: Susan E. Morse; PRODUCTION: Robert Greenhut – Charles H. Joffe – Orion Pictures
CAST: Woody Allen (Leonard Zelig), Mia Farrow (Eudora Fletcher), Susan Sontag, Irving Howe, Saul Bellow and Bruno Bettelheim (themselves)
RUNNING TIME: 84 minutes

1984 BROADWAY DANNY ROSE
DIRECTOR: Woody Allen; SUBJECT AND SCREENPLAY: Woody Allen; PHOTOGRAPHY: Gordon Willis (black and white, Panavision); ART DIRECTOR: Mel Bourne; MUSIC: Dick Hyman, plus songs by Nick Apollo Forte; EDITOR: Susan E. Morse; PRODUCTION: Robert Greenhut – Charles H. Joffe – Orion Pictures
CAST: Woody Allen (Danny Rose), Mia Farrow (Tina Vitale), Nick Apollo Forte (Lou Canova), Milton Berle, Will Jordan, Sandy Baron, Jack Rollins, Morty Gunty, Corbett Monica, Jackie Gayle and Howard Storm (themselves).
RUNNING TIME: 86 minutes

1985 THE PURPLE ROSE OF CAIRO
DIRECTOR: Woody Allen; SUBJECT AND SCREENPLAY: Woody Allen; PHOTOGRAPHY: Gordon Willis (black and white/colour); ART DIRECTOR: Stuart Wurtzel; MUSIC: Dick Hyman and songs from the repertoire; EDITOR: Susan E. Morse; PRODUCTION: Robert Greenhut – Charles H. Joffe – Orion Pictures
CAST: Mia Farrow (Cecilia), Jeff Daniels (Tom Baxter/Gil Shepherd), Danny Aiello (Monk), Stephanie Farrow (Cecilia's sister), John Wood (Jason), Van Johnson (Larry), Zoe Caldwell (Countess), Milo O'Shea (Father Donnelly), Ed Herrmann (Henry), Deborah Rush (Rita)
RUNNING TIME: 81 minutes

1986 HANNAH AND HER SISTERS
DIRECTOR: Woody Allen; SUBJECT AND SCREENPLAY: Woody Allen; PHOTOGRAPHY: Carlo Di Palma (Technicolor); ART DIRECTOR: Stuart Wurtzel; MUSIC: music and songs from the repertoire; EDITOR: Susan E. Morse; PRODUCTION: Robert Greenhut – Rollins and Joffe – Orion Pictures
CAST: Woody Allen (Mickey), Michael Caine (Eliot), Mia Farrow (Hannah), Barbara Hershey (Lee), Dianne Wiest (Holly), Max Von Sydow (Frederick), Carrie Fisher (April), Lloyd Nolan (Father), Maureen O'Sullivan (Mother), Daniel Stern (Dusty), Sam Waterston (Architect), Tony Roberts (Mickey's friend)
RUNNING TIME: 106 minutes

1987 RADIO DAYS
DIRECTOR: Woody Allen; SUBJECT AND SCREENPLAY: Woody Allen; PHOTOGRAPHY: Carlo Di Palma (colour, Panavision); ART DIRECTOR: Santo Loquasto; MUSIC: Dick Hyman and music from the repertoire; EDITOR: Susan E. Morse; PRODUCTION: Robert Greenhut – Rollins and Joffe – Orion Pictures
CAST: Seth Green (Joe), Julie Kavner (his Mother), Michael Tucker (his Father), Dianne Wiest (Aunt Bea), Mia Farrow (Sally White), Danny Aiello (Rocco), and including Diane Keaton, Tony Roberts and Jeff Daniels
RUNNING TIME: 88 minutes

RECORDS

WOODY ALLEN. Colpix CP 488, 1964.

WOODY ALLEN, VOL. 2. Colpix CP 518, 1965.

THE THIRD WOODY ALLEN ALBUM. Capitol ST 2986, 1968.

WOODY ALLEN – THE NIGHT CLUB YEARS, 1964–1968. United Artists UA 9968, 1976.

WOODY ALLEN – STAND-UP COMIC, 1964–1968. United Artists UA-LA 849–J2, 1978.

BOOKS

DON'T DRINK THE WATER – A Comedy in Two Acts. Samuel French, New York 1967.

PLAY IT AGAIN, SAM – A Romantic Comedy in Three Acts. Samuel French, New York 1969.

GETTING EVEN. Random House, New York 1971.

WITHOUT FEATHERS. Random House, New York 1975.

DEATH – A Comedy in One Act. Samuel French, New York 1975.

GOD – A Comedy in One Act. Samuel French, New York 1975.

SIDE EFFECTS. Random House, New York 1980.

FOUR FILMS OF WOODY ALLEN – Annie Hall, Interiors, Manhattan, Stardust Memories. Random House, New York 1982.

PLAYS

DON'T DRINK THE WATER – A Comedy in Two Acts. First performance in New York (Morosco Theatre), 17 November 1966. Director: Stanley Prager.

PLAY IT AGAIN, SAM – A Comedy in Three Acts. First performance, in New York (Broadhurst Theatre), 12 February 1969. Director: Joseph Hardy.

THE FLOATING LIGHTBULB – A Drama in Two Acts. First performance, in New York (Vivian Beaumont Theatre), 27 April 1981. Director: Ulu Grosbard.

BIBLIOGRAPHICAL NOTES

It would be impossible to list here all the vast number of articles, reviews and interviews published both in the press and specialist publications on Woody Allen in his various creative guises.

With regard particularly to the cinema, the following works should be mentioned: 'Woody Allen', by Robert Mundy and Stephen Mamber (Cinema, vol.7 n.3, winter 1972–73); 'The Basic Woody Allen Joke', by Richard Schickel (New York Times Magazine, 7/1/1973); 'Guilty, With An Explanation', by Penelope Gilliatt (The New Yorker, 4/2/1974); 'Take Woody Allen – Please!', by Leonard Maltin (Film Comment, vol.10 n.2, March-April 1974); 'Woody Allen is Feeling Better', by Bernard Drew (American Film, vol.2 n.7, May 1977); 'The Autobiography of Woody Allen', by Michael Dempsey (Film Comment, vol.15 n.3, May-June, 1979); 'A Little Faith in People', by Richard Corlis (id.); 'Woody Allen's Love Letter to Diane Keaton', by Jack Foley (Bright Light, vol.3 n.1, 1980); 'Woody Allen', by Robert F. Moss (SR, November 1980).

In French critical literature, the following should be noted: Le rire et la culture (le citoyen Allen et Spinoza)', by Robert Benayoun (Positif, n.199, Novembre 1977); 'Portrait de l'artiste en masochiste serein', by Emmanuel Carrière (id.); 'L'un dit gestion de ça, voire', by Jean Funck (Positif, n.215, Février 1979); 'Un désespoir d'humour', by Robert Benayoun (Positif, n.222, Septembre 1979); 'Deux entretiens avec Woody Allen', by Robert Benayoun (id.); 'Manhattan, ou le temps retrouvé' and 'La femme, le WASP et le schlemiel', by Gilles Cèbe (Écran, n.83, 15/9/79).

Among the Italian contributions, the preface written by Umberto Eco for the book of Woody Allen's writings Saperla lunga – Getting Even (Bompiani, Milan 1973) is of particular importance; the chapter on Woody Allen by Franco La Polla in 'Il nuovo cinema americano' (Marsilio, Venice 1978); the reviews of Annie Hall, Interiors, Manhattan, Stardust Memories, A Midsummer Night's Sex Comedy and Zelig by Emanuela Martini (Cineforum nos.177, 186, 191, 202, 219, 229); 'Allen; il Modello e La Superficie', by Leonardo Quaresima (Cinema e cinema, n.29, October-December 1981); the reviews of Annie Hall, Interiors, Manhattan, Stardust Memories, A Midsummer Night's Sex Comedy and Zelig (Letture, 77–818, 79–223, 80–51, 81–329, 82–798, 84–69), as well as 'Manhattan, una commedia fuori moda' (Cinemasessanta, n.130, November-December 1979) by Gianalberto Bendazzi.

Lastly, the graduate thesis Aspects of Woody Allen's Cinema written by Pino Gaeta (Istituto Universitario orientale de Napoli, academic year 1979–80, supervisor Professor Mino Argentieri) should also be recommended.

Publications in book form:
On Being Funny – Woody Allen and Comedy, by Eric Lax (Charterhouse, New York 1975)
Woody Allen – Clown Prince of the American Humor, by Bill Adler and Jeffrey Feinman (Pinnacle, New York 1975)
Woody Allen by Giannalberto Bendazzi (La Nuova Italia, Florence 1976)
Woody Allen's Play It Again, Sam, edited by Richard J. Anobile (Grosset & Dunlap, New York 1977)
Woody Allen – A Biography, by Lee Guthrie (Drake, New York 1978)
Loser Take All – The Comic Art of Woody Allen, by Maurice Yacowar (Ungar, New York 1979)
Woody Allen, by Michel Lebrun (PAC, Paris 1979)
Woody Allen, by Myles Palmer (Proteus, New York 1980)
Woody Allen, by Gilles Cèbe (Veyrier, Paris 1981)
Love, Sex, Death, and the Meaning of Life – Woody Allen's Comedy, by Foster Hirsch (McGraw-Hill, New York 1981)
The Magic of Woody Allen, by Diane Jacobs (Robson, London 1982)
Woody Allen – Joking Aside, by Gerald McKnight (W.H. Allen, London 1982)
Woody Allen: His Films and Career, by Douglas Brode (Citadel Press, Seacaucus 1985)
Woody Allen, by Christian Dureau, (PAC, Paris 1985)
Woody Allen, au delà du langage, by Robert Benayoun (Herscher, Paris 1985)
Die vielen Gesichter des Woody Allen, by Wolfgang J. Fuchs (Taschen, Köln 1986)
Woody Allen on Location, by Thierry de Navacelle (William Morrow & Co., New York 1986)

INDEX OF NAMES
(bold figures denote illustration)

Aiello, Danny 186, **187**, 189
Akhmatova, Anna 101
Alpert, Hollis 138
Andress, Ursula 15, 16
Ansen, David 201
Anspach, Susan 74
Antonioni, Michelangelo 23, 33, 83, 197
Armstrong, Louis 41, 136, 146, 157
Astaire, Fred 188, 189

Bacharach, Burt 15
Bacon, Francis 37
Baer, Max 5
Ballard, Kaye 10
Baker, Josephine 173
Barnes, Clive 18, 25
Baron, Sandy 180, **180**, 185
Barrault, Marie-Christine 149, **150**
Barry, Jack 77
Barthelme, Donald 32
Base, Ron 188
Beatty, Warren 15
Bellow, Saul 40, 177
Benson, Sheila 203
Bergman, Ingmar 5, 21, 23, 25, 33, 38, 40, 41, 61, 102, 103, 121, 122, 124, 125, 132, 147, 152, 158, 197
Bergman, Ingrid 70
Berle, Milton 12, 181
Bernstein, Leonard 158
Bernstein, Walter 25, 158
Bertolucci, Bernardo 32, 83
Bettelheim, Bruno 177
Bogart, Humphrey 18, 29, 32, 33, 66, 67, 69, 70, 75
Bogdanovich, Peter 20, 32, 144
Boll, Heinrich 132
Bonaparte, Napoleon 29, 103, 104
Boone, Pat 10
Bourne, Mel 128
Braddock, Jim 5
Brando, Marlon 41, 136
Brickman, Marshall 26
Broccoli, Albert R. 16
Brooks, Mel 10, 12, 38, 101
Brown, Clarence 5
Brown, Joe E. 190
Bruce, Lenny 13
Burrows, Abe 9
Byrne, Anne 132, 135, 142

Caesar, Sid 10, 12, 22
Cagney, James 173
Caine, Michael 27, 192, **194**, 197
Caldwell, Zoe 191
Camus, Albert 40
Canby, Vincent 20, 21, 22, 25, 188, 198
Cantor, Eddie 12
Capra, Frank 5
Capucine 15
Carey, Leah 200, 202
Carnera, Primo 5
Carney, Art 10
Carradine, John 78, 79, 84
Cavett, Dick 14
Cezanne, Paul 136
Channing, Carol 10
Chaplin, Charlie 5, 29, 30, 38, 41, 61, 89, 103, 183, 185
Chapman, Lonnie 51
Chekhov, Anton 25, 142
Cherrie, Nettea 6
Cholem-Aléikhem 40
Clair, Rene 61
Clark, Mike 199
Connery, Sean 16

Coolidge, Calvin 168, **168**
Cooper, Gary 33
Cosby, Bill 14
Cosell, Howard 54, 58, 59, 61
Coursodon, Jean-Pierre 29
Cummings, E. E. 192
Curtiz, Michael 32, 70

Daney, Serge 117
Daniels, Jeff 186, 188, 190, **190**
David O., Alber 8, 9
Davila, Diana 73
Davy, Dick 14
Dean, James 33
Delvaux, André 152
Dempsey, Jack 168, 171
Denby, David 203
De Niro, Robert 142
Dickens, Charles 201
Dietrich, Marlene 5
DiPalma, Carlo 197, 203
Disney, Walt 158
Donner, Clive 15, **15**
Dostoyevsky, Fiodor 101
Doumanian, Jean 26
Dovjenko, Aleksandr 147
Dulles, John Foster 14
Duvall, Shelley 121

Eisenhower, Dwight 14, 111
Eisenstein, Serge 32, 102, 103

Farrow, Mia 20, 26, 158, 161, 173, 179, 181, 183, **184**, 185, 186, 189, 190, 192, 193, 195, 197, 202
Farrow, Stephanie 187
Feiffer, Jules 30
Feldman, Charles K. 14, 15, 16
Fellini, Federico 5, 23, 25, 38, 40, 152, 185, 190, 203
Ferrer, José 158, **159**, 167
Fields, W. C. 147
Fisher, Carrie 192, 196
Fitzgerald, Francis Scott 132, 179
Flaubert, Gustave 41, 136
Fleischer, Richard 83
Fleming, Ian 16
Fletcher, Eudora 36
Fletcher, Mari 68
Ford, John 5
Forte, Nick Apollo 180, 183, 185
Freud, Sigmund 14, 40, 110

Gable, Clark 5, 16
Garbo, Greta 5
Gauguin, Paul 36
Gayle, Jackie 180, 181
Gelb, Arthur 13
Gelbart, Larry 10
Georges-Picot, Olga 96
Gershwin, George 5, 132, 144, 145
Green, Seth 200, 201
Grierson, John 203
Godard, Jean-Luc 32
Gogol, Nicholas Vassilievitch 100
Goldman, Albert 10
Gould, Harold 97, 102
Gregory, Dick 14
Griffith, Kristin 127
Grosbard, Ulu 25
Gunty, Morty 180

Hackett, Buddy 10, 12, 161
Hagerty, Julie 158
Hall, Herb 31
Hample, Stuart 24

Hardy, Joseph 18
Hardy, Oliver 35, 36, 38
Harper, Jessica 149, 150
Hayworth, Rita 140
Heller, Joseph 40
Hemingway, Ernest 35, 199
Hemingway, Mariel 132, 136, 137, 140, **140**, 143
Hennesy, Dale 83
Hershey, Barbara 192, 193, 197
Hillaire, Marcel 45
Himes, Geoffrey 203
Hitler, Adolf 5, 35, 40, 170, 171, 177
Hoffman, Dustin 142
Hoover, Herbert 168, 169
Hope, Bob 8, 13, 100, 103
Howe, Irving 177
Hunter, Stephen 199
Hurt, Mary Beth 122, 131
Huxley, Aldous 92
Hyde, Jacqueline 48
Hyman, Dick 173, 203

Inagaki, Hiroshi 147

Jacobi, Lou 18, 77, 83, 84, **84**
Jancso, Miklos 103
Joffe, Charles 12, 13, 14, 20, 50
Johns, Jaspers 32
Johnson, Van 191
Jordan, Richard 124
Jordan, Will 180, **180**
Josephson, Erland 124
Jung, Carl Gustav 14, 40, 132

Kael, Pauline 25
Kafka, Franz 40
Kallen, Lucille 10
Kaye, Danny 12, 29, 100
Kaye, Sammy 8
Keaton, Buster 20, 29, 30, 38, 62, 89, 92, 108, 190
Keaton, Diane 18, 20, 22, 25, 26, 40, 69, 71, 75, 86, 91, 94, 96, 97, 106, 107, 110, 116, 123, 131, 132, **133**, 142, 199
Kavner, Julie 200
Kennedy, John 111
Kerr, Walter 18, 25
Kierkegaard, Soren 32, 40
Kissinger, Henry 22
Klein, Robert 14
Konigsberg, Alan Stewart (Woody Allen) 5, 7, 8, 9
Konigsberg, Letty 6
Konigsberg, Martin 6
Kroll, Jack 26
Kurland, Jeffrey 197, 203

Lacy, Jerry 18, 68, 75
La Guardia, Fiorello 5
Lang, Fritz 48
Langdon, Harry 89
Lasser, Louise 17, 26, 64, 82
Lasser, S. Jay 17
Laughton, Charles 5
Laurel, Stan 13, 36, 38, 48
Lemmon, Jack 190
Lewis, Jerry 12, 23, 29, 36, 38, 40
Lichtenstein, Roy 32
Lindbergh, Charles 168
Lippin, Renée 149, 200
Lloyd, Frank 5
Lloyd, Harold 20, 29, 89
Lombardo, Guy 8, 198
Loquasto, Santo 165, 203
Lubitsch, Ernst 142

Lucas, George 20
Lumet, Baruch 81

MacLaine, Shirley 14
Magerman, William 200, 202
Magris, Claudio 40
Mahler, Gustav 132
Malamud, Bernard 40
Malle, Louis 32
Mamoulian, Rouben 5
Marcovicci, Andrea 23
Margolin, Janet 47
Marshall, E. G. 125
Marthen, Joe 24
Marx Brothers 56, 21, 23, 30, 48, 65, 193, 195, 203
Marx, Groucho 20, 41, 61, 110, 136, 146
Marx, Harpo 18, 108
Mata Hari 16
May, Elaine 14
Mays, Willie 6, 136, 146
McCarthy, Joseph 14
McCarthy, Todd 188
McLuhan, Marshall 121
McMurty, Larry 138
McRae, Heather 80
Mendelssohn, Felix 158
Miller, Arthur 25
Miller, Glen 203
Miller, Henry 5
Miranda, Carmen 203
Mitchell, John 22
Molière 195
Monica, Corbett 180, 180
Monicelli, Mario 83
Monroe, Marilyn 16, 148
Montalban, Carlos 59
Moore, Garry 13
Morris, Howard 22
Mostel, Josh 200
Mozart, Wolfgang Amadeus 41, 96
Munk, Jonathan 39
Murphy, Michael 24, 26, 135, 142
Musatti, Cesare 41

Nachman, Gerald 198
Newman, Joy 200
Nichols, Mike 14
Niven, David 16
Nixon, Richard 14, 22, 48, 92
Nolan, Lloyd 192, 194

Odets, Clifford 25
O'Neill, Eugene 143, 168, 170
O'Sullivan, Maureen 192, 194
Ophuls, Marcel 121
Ormandy, Eugene 158
Orwell, George 92

O'Toole, Peter 15, 36

Paar, Jack 10
Pacino, Al 22
Page, Geraldine 123, 131
Podhoretz, John 201
Porter, Cole 84, 168, 203
Prager, Stanley 18
Prentiss, Paula 15
Prokofiev, Serguei 103

Quayle, Anthony 76, 83

Rampling, Charlotte 149, 151
Randall, Tony 83
Rauschenberg, Robert 32
Redgrave, Lynn 83
Reed, Rex 188
Renoir, Jean 147
Reynolds, Burt 83
Richardson, Tony 61
Ritt, Martin 25
Roberts, Tony 18, 26, 75, 112, 158, 161, 201
Rogers, Ginger 188, 189
Rollins, Jack 12, 14, 50, 180, 181
Roosevelt, Franklin Delano 5
Rosen, Harlene 9, 10, 14
Rosenblum, Ralph 20
Ross, Herbert 22, 72
Roth, Philip 40
Runyon, Damon 183, 189
Ruth, Babe 5

Sahl, Mort 14
Salaman, Julie 203
Sanchez, Ref 78
Saperstein, Henry 17
Sarris, Andrew 26, 142, 201
Sauter, Michael 199, 203
Schickel, Richard 25, 26, 33, 188
Schneider, Romy 15, 15, 17
Schumacher, Joel 128
Scooler, Zvee 98
Scorsese, Martin 20, 32
Seale, Bobby 65
Sellers, Peter 15, 15, 16, 17, 26
Sennett, Mack 29
Shakespeare, William 158
Shanker, Albert 36
Shriner, Herb 10
Simon, Danny 10
Simon, Neil 10
Sinatra, Frank 136
Sinclair, Bob 18
Sontag, Susan 168
Spielberg, Steven 20
Spillane, Mickey 32
Stallone, Sylvester 55, 56

Stapleton, Maureen 131
Stark, Susan 203
Steenburgen, Mary 158, 159
Stefanov, Vassil 158
Stein, Gertrude 199
Stein, Joseph 10
Steinbeck, John 5
Stern, Daniel 194
Sternberg, Josef von 5
Stevenson, Adlai 111
Stewart, Mike 10
Storm, Howard 180, 181
Streep, Meryl 133, 134
Streisand, Barbra 17
Sturges, Preston 190
Swift, Jonathan 62
Swindell, Larry 201

Tchekhov, Anton
Thomson, David 201
Tolkan, James 107
Tolkin, Mel 10
Tolstoy, Leon Nikolaievitch 101
Toto 89
Toulouse-Lautrec, Henri de 36
Travis, Bernie 14
Truffaut, François 32
Tucker, Michael 200

Ullmann, Liv 124

Van Gogh, Vincent 36
Varda, Agnès 32
Verniere, James 188, 201
Viva 72
Voltaire 62
Von Sydow, Max 192, 194

Waller, Fats 173
Warrilow, David 202
Waterston, Sam 124, 192, 196
Welles, Orson 16, 199, 201
Widerberg, Bo 165
Weist, Diane 27, 192, 193, 197, 200, 2
Wilde, Oscar 38
Wilder, Gene 76, 83, 84, 85
Williams, Tennessee 25
Willis, Gordon 26, 121, 143, 158, 188
Wilson, Dooley 70
Wilson, Earl 8
Winchell, Walter 8
Winger, Debra 190
Wolf, William 188

Youngman, Henny 13

Zdanov, Andre 101
Zenor, Susanne 75
Zola, Emile 36